LIVE BY THE SPIRIT

The Parish Church
of
St. Mary Magdalene,
Frinton-on-Sea.

By the same author

PENTECOSTAL ANGLICANS
A PEOPLE FOR HIS PRAISE

LIVE BY THE SPIRIT

JOHN GUNSTONE

HODDER AND STOUGHTON
LONDON SYDNEY AUCKLAND TORONTO

British Library Cataloguing in Publication Data

Gunstone, John
  Live by the Spirit.
  1. Holy Spirit
  I. Title
  231'.3   BT121.2

ISBN 0 340 36146 8

Hodder and Stoughton Editorial Office: 47 Bedford Square, London WC1B 3DP

Contents

Introduction

Some years ago in the church press there was a picture of a crowd celebrating Pentecost in Trafalgar Square. The National Gallery formed a back-cloth to the scene. In the front of the picture were two Franciscan brothers leaping joyfully into the air, their habits flying to reveal bare legs and sandals.

According to the caption one was shouting to the other, 'You'd have thought this would have gone with the job!'

There is much misunderstanding about the operation of the Holy Spirit in a Christian's life. Some see him only in moments of ecstasy, as the picture suggested. Others see him working hiddenly in the daily duties of a conscientious churchman. And others limit his manifestations to extra-ordinary spiritual gifts.

It is because of these misunderstandings that I've written a book about living by the Spirit in everyday life.

I've begun by exploring how we come to believe in God as Father, Son and Holy Spirit. To do this in the first chapter I've had to rely on my own experience of coming to faith because that – as far as I can remember it – is a convenient source of illustrative material. I know accounts of personal experience are subjective and therefore somewhat suspect, but I wanted to ground what I said in what we actually think and feel about our relationships with God. Perhaps you can use my account to reflect on your own.

In the second and following chapters I've relied more on the experiences of others, especially their response to the Word of God as they heard him speaking to them through the scriptures in different ages. Church tradition tends to be regarded as a stumbling-block to discipleship these days. It's blamed for all kinds of hindrances to the work of the Holy Spirit. But that is often because we do not look for the right things in it. We get confused by the tradition instead of being enlightened by what it represented: Christians' response to the Word of God in their own times and circumstances as they believed the Spirit was leading them. That is where the lesson is to be found.

Church tradition comes to us in different forms – customs and disciplines, the rules of the religious orders and the writings of men and women wise in the ways of God. But one source is easily accessible: the prayer and ritual of the Church's liturgy. When men and women worship, they express what they believe God is saying to them and doing through them in Jesus Christ by his Spirit; and the liturgy hands their beliefs on to us for our encouragement. That is why I have made use of quotations from the liturgy in most chapters.

Obviously a subject like this can only be treated in general terms. Our lives vary so much. But the unity of the Spirit is such that we should be able to help one another, even if you and I do live in very different circumstances. It is in that hope that I've written this book.

At the beginning of my motorists' atlas of Great Britain there is a route-planning map. Before I work out a journey, I first look up this map to get a rough idea of the roads I should take and the towns I should pass through. Only after I've done that do I turn to the more detailed drawings on other pages for further information. This book is offered as a sort of route-planning map for Christian disciples. For more detailed guidance you must look elsewhere.

John Gunstone

CHAPTER 1

Seasons of Grace

Why am I a Christian?

A straightforward answer to that question would be, I'm a Christian because I believe Jesus Christ is my Lord and Saviour.

But even as I write these words, I'm conscious of what they don't reveal.

I've written, *I believe*. But how far is my belief my own? When I make a decision as a Christian, trusting that I'm being obedient to God, is that decision really mine, or have I reached it because of the influences I've absorbed from other people? Have I been emotionally and mentally programmed into belief through heredity, upbringing and environment?

And I've written, *Jesus Christ is my Lord and Saviour*. But what do I mean by those words? What is my concept of Jesus Christ and where did that concept come from? How do I understand his lordship and his saving work as it applies to me? And how do I grasp what Jesus said about his heavenly Father?

Looking back, I don't think I can claim I became a believing Christian until after I left home to go to Durham University when I was 18. Until then, my Christian faith and practice depended heavily on my parents' example. With them I was more of a catechumen – a probationer Christian.

I had no memorable conversion experience. Rather, belief in Jesus Christ became necessary because I had to make choices away from the immediate influence of my father and mother (a strong influence: I was an only child). Christ's invitation, 'Follow me', became real and relevant in the process of making decisions about my ideas, my conduct, my relationships and my future.

What did influence me was the friendship of other young Christians in the university, many of them were more mature in their faith than I was. Meeting them I felt the inadequacy of my own 'churchianity'. I began to read the Bible regularly and to pray with a sense of purpose.

A sermon during a college retreat challenged me. It was an exposition of Matthew 10: 39, 'He who finds his life will lose it, and he who loses his life for my sake will find it.' How important was Jesus Christ in my life? Was I willing to put his will before my own? Perhaps if there was a moment of conversion during my years at the university, this was it.

Baptism, confirmation and first Communion would have been very appropriate for me during that retreat if I had not received the sacraments of Christian initiation earlier. In some ways I regret I have no memory of my baptism. Yet the traditional practice of the Church of England in christening me as an infant had this to be said for it: it expressed sacramentally the influence of a Christian home.

The beginnings of our faith in God are laid down from the moment we are born (or perhaps before). In being handled, caressed, played with and talked to as babies, we are made to feel we matter. We become conscious of ourselves as persons. To be loved as a child is powerfully associated with the satisfaction of our needs – hunger, comfort, sleep, companionship. It is a very self-centred experience.

Later, we have to learn that we are not the centre of our parents' universe – or, indeed, of anyone else's. Other people matter as well. In a Christian home an awareness of God develops, as One who matters more than the others.

Then we learn by imitation. Love was demonstrated by the way my parents treated one another. They weren't faultless. They had their ups and downs. But between them there was a mutual trust and a willingness to sacrifice self for the other that was the first manifestation of love in my experience. Being loved myself, and seeing them love one another, prepared me for such lessons as, 'God is love, and whoever abides in love abides in God, and God abides in him' (1 John 4: 16).

That text is usually interpreted to mean God's abiding presence in the heart of the individual believer. Yet it is equally applicable to the experience of being loved within a believing community. To give its members first-hand experience of being loved is the fundamental ministry of any Christian family. It prepares them to recognise and to respond to the love of God. We shall see later how this experience is behind the Christian understanding of the family as a church-in-miniature.

It is said that we cannot love others unless we have known what it is to be loved ourselves. I would add a supplement to that: unless we know what it is to be loved ourselves, we shall need inner healing before we can truly believe God loves us. Those early experiences of parental affection, forgiveness and guidance, create in us a model which helps us later to develop our concept of God as our heavenly Father.

Notice I used the word *parental*, not paternal. This is because experience of a mother's love is as important as experience of a father's love in creating this model. In the story of creation, the female as well as the male reflects the image of God: 'Let us make man in our image, after our likeness... So God created man in his own image, in the image of God he created him; male and female he created them' (Gen. 1: 26-7).

There are two ways of interpreting this text. One is that the mother-figure points to God just as powerfully as the father-figure in our early lives. Certain Christian mystics took this idea up. Julian of Norwich, for example, wrote that Jesus Christ is a revelation of God as Mother to us, for it is through him that we are brought to new birth. Other writers discerned a female principle in the person of the Holy Spirit, prompted by fact that the word for *spirit* in Hebrew is a feminine noun. More recently the theme has emerged in

contemporary feminist theology, which refers to God as
'She'. If we are born into a single-parent family, we can still
experience the human love that prepares us to receive the
love of God, even if we've never known a father.

The other way of looking at the Genesis text is to see the
image of God, not just in the mother- and the father-figures
but in the *relationship* between the mother and the father.
This, I think, is what happened in my case. It was the way my
parents expressed their love for one another in dozens of
different, everyday things that pointed me towards the
loving heavenly Father.

Belief in Jesus Christ emerged within that wider
experience. When I was young I listened to, and later read
for myself, the story of Jesus. A huge family bible belonging
to my grandparents was a favourite book. For a long time
the nineteenth-century etchings remained in my memory
when I read the scriptures.

Although the 'Our Father' was one of the first prayers I
learned, it was Jesus I pictured when I said it. When I saw my
parents kneeling at their bedside, it was Jesus I assumed they
were speaking to. Jesus was the someone who mattered in
our house.

Worship was the first item on the agenda for Sunday
mornings. I cannot remember a time when I was not taken to
church. The pew we usually occupied in St Lawrence's
Church, Long Eaton, became as familiar to me as my own
bedroom.

St Lawrence's was a bulwark of the Anglo-Catholic
tradition of the Church of England, and the way worship
was conducted impressed itself on my childish mind. How
wonderful Jesus Christ must be for us to invoke his name
with hymns and prayers, candles and incense, processions
and genuflections!

I looked forward with excitement to Christmas – not just
for the presents but also for the eucharist in church when the
bambino was solemnly blessed and taken in procession to
the crib. Good Friday was an awesome affair, with mournful

music, the reading of the Passion, and the emptiness of the church stripped of ornaments. Easter Day, by contrast, was glorious with white vestments, resurrection hymns, flowers and spring sunshine. The liturgical year, punctiliously observed in St Lawrence's, made me feel that Jesus was not just a character in a story but One who lives among us now.

Among other religions experiences in my pre-student days, two stand out in significance.

One was the discipline of going to confession. In Anglo-Catholic parishes, candidates for confirmation were expected to make their first confession to a priest, and this I duly did, kneeling at a prayer desk in St Lawrence's. On the curtain in front of me (behind which the vicar was sitting in cassock, cotta and purple stole) was pinned a black and silver crucifix. Although I was only 9 years of age, it dawned on me that the forgiveness of my sins was possible only because of Christ's death on the cross.

The veil that surrounds the mystery of the atonement was momentarily lifted in that experience. The discipline of going to confession, established in childhood, has done much to assure me that in Jesus I really am accepted as a redeemed son by the heavenly Father.

The other experience was when I was a teenager. During the war we lived near Mount St Bernard Abbey in Leicestershire, and when there was no service in the little Anglican mission on the estate, we used to walk on Sunday mornings through the lanes of Charnwood Forest to attend mass in the abbey church.

The service was certainly inspiring. The ritual of the Cistercian order is austere, and the celebration was stripped of all but the simplest ceremonial, accompanied by plainsong. But it was the deep peace of the place that drew me. Mount St Bernard is a Trappist monastery, and the silence enfolds not only the community's buildings but also the fields around them. On summer evenings I used to cycle alone to the abbey and sit in the Neo-Gothic church with its white oil-lamp flickering near the tabernacle on the high altar.

In that intense quietness I became aware of God's presence in a mode I had not known before.

It was at such times as these that a boyish notion of being a priest developed into a conviction that God was calling me to be ordained in the Church of England.

Parental love, the sacramental life of the Church, the encounter with God in the silence – these were some of the things that formulated my concept of God and of Jesus Christ, and it was out of this background that I went up to Durham.

The years following the end of the war, although bleak with economic cutbacks, were years of hope and confidence for the Church. The overthrow of Nazism seemed to symbolise a victory over evil. Men demobbed from the armed forces were crowding into the theological colleges to train for the ministry. New churches were being built to replace those that had been bombed and to serve new areas. Many believed God was opening up new possibilities for the Church's mission in this country.

This confidence was reflected in the teaching of the distinguished theologians who were in Durham when I was a student. Their biblical theology seemed to reinforce the traditional Catholic-Anglicanism in which I had been brought up.

Commitment to the Lord for me meant remaining faithful to the belief that he was calling me to be ordained. Other opportunities presented themselves. Various friends were planning to embark on what seemed to be more exciting and certainly more lucrative careers. In those days offering myself for the Anglican ministry felt like a sacrifical step.

My obedience was tested during the years that followed my graduation when I was doing my national service. For the first time in my life I was flung into a totally secular environment. The British army of occupation in post-war

Austria was a society of extremes: genuine comradeship, generosity and concern for one another jostled alongside such blasphemy, immorality and dishonesty as I had never met before.

Yet the darkness of what was evil made the light of what was good so much brighter. Those years gave me glimpses of God active in his world far beyond the bounds of the baptised community. Among men with little or no Christian background, I met the care that pointed me to Jesus Christ. Years later, when I became familiar with the prophecy, 'And it shall come to pass afterward, that I will pour out my spirit on all flesh' (Joel 2: 28), I interpreted it in terms of what God can do through all men and women, of different faiths as well as of none, largely because of what I first experienced in the army.

I was demobbed in 1950 to commence training for ordination at the College of the Resurrection, Mirfield.

The College is staffed by members of the Community of the Resurrection, an Anglican religious order. Although as students we lived separately from the community ('the Dads', as they were affectionately called out of their hearing), the priests and laymen in it had a considerable influence on us. We worshipped with them in the community church each day, we listened to their lectures and sermons, we went to them for tutorials and spiritual advice, we chatted to them in the common room and during walks.

And we watched their comings and goings as they fulfilled their ministry in Britain and in South Africa. Here were men who used to be students like us, who had been parish priests as we hoped to be, and yet who had surrendered their independence, their possessions, their hopes of a family and much else that we took for granted, to serve God in a lifestyle that strikingly demonstrated certain Gospel precepts. Perhaps that was the most influential lesson they offered us.

When I went to Mirfield, my concept of God and of Jesus Christ was still simple and uncomplicated. Theological debates at Durham had not disturbed the foundations of my faith. Academic study had been largely detached from my personal life. But in the theological college, this changed. What we read and discussed caused long questioning about what we believed. We engaged in earnest and often heated debates about God, about the incarnation, about the Church, about moral decisions and many other matters.

Thinking through our faith is necessary discipline. God does not want us to put our minds into cold storage after we have turned to him. We build on sand if we base our Christian discipleship on a few spiritual experiences, or on doctrines that we've learned in the past and now refuse to test in the light of reason. God may choose what is foolish in the world to shame the wise, but that doesn't mean he wants the foolish to stop thinking!

Yet there is a massive difference between doing such a rethink by oneself and doing it in the fellowship of a believing and worshipping community. As students we were shaken by the philosophical, psychological and sociological studies which seemed to prove that our attitudes and behaviour were dominated by a determinism that made the possibility of free choice an illusion. But because we were in the midst of a community of believers, academic conundrums never overwhelmed us. They remained a matter of dialogue between the Church and the world, not at the heart of our life which was constantly directed towards the love of God by the older men around us.

My Mirfield experience had its limitations. In spite of the community's ecumenical openness, we students were convinced that evangelicals and other Christian traditions had little to offer us. We believed the country would become more Christian when more people became Anglo-Catholic. That was a common assumption among high churchmen in those days!

Yet the community and the college helped me to relate the Gospel to the Church's mission in the world, and they enabled me to establish a discipline of daily prayer which has

remained with me ever since. I left Mirfield with a belief in
God and in the saving work of Jesus Christ that had been
much enriched through worshipping and learning among
them.

I thought I had a pretty efficient knowledge of what I had
to do as a priest in the Church of England. Ordination was
my commissioning. The teaching and the sacraments of the
Church were my resources. God and I would be able to
achieve much together!

Work as a curate in Walthamstow and Forest Gate and as
a vicar in Romford did little, as far as I can tell, to lead me to
greater spiritual maturity. Conducting an endless round of
services each week, preaching two or three times on
Sundays, presiding at meetings and worrying about raising
money, baptising babies and burying the dead – it all seemed
far removed from what I had imagined. People weren't
converted to Anglo-Catholicism, or even to Christianity, in
the numbers I had expected.

Now and then there were moments to celebrate –
confirmations, festival services, missions, retreats. A few
gave their lives to the Lord each year. I felt I was being used
as God's servant in my involvement with parishioners' hopes
and disappointments, tragedies and joys. And, above all,
there was the privilege of being with men and women whose
devotion to Jesus Christ was far greater than mine. Meeting
the Lord in them was a humbling and thrilling experience.

By the time I had been ten years in the ordained ministry,
however, I felt I was growing away from God. My Mirfield
days seemed to be the peak of my discipleship. The
theological turmoil of the 'sixties depressed me. I was angry
with the Church for failing to fulfil my expectations of her.
A staleness and cynicism crept into my attitude towards my
parochial work.

A wise priest told a friend he had been disturbed by some
things I had written in the church press. The friend passed
the comment on to me. I was startled. I was not aware that
my articles revealed an impoverishment in my faith. But that

is what the priest had discerned.

I had yet to learn that one of the risks an author takes is that of revealing more of himself to his readers than he intends!

In my spiritual pilgrimage until this time I had had little concept of God the Holy Spirit. I'd joined in hymns to the Spirit. I'd invoked his guidance at the beginning of sermons and addresses. I'd heard the bishop pray for the Spirit when I'd been confirmed and ordained. And I'd studied heresies associated with pneumatology!

But somehow I never really felt that I *knew* the Holy Spirit. Trying to preach on Whitsunday each year was an embarrassment. I just couldn't think of anything worthwhile to say. I rationalised the events narrated in Acts 2 as a dramatic mystical experience that was unique in the life of the apostolic Church, and I warned confirmation candidates not to expect anything like it today. The basic textbook on Christian doctrine which I had used from my college days contained one brief chapter on the Spirit. I assumed that what the New Testament taught about spiritual gifts (and I wasn't very clear about that, anyway) was now to be found in the sacraments, orders and liturgy of the Church. Charisms had become routinised.

If anyone had asked me (which they never did) how to receive more of the Holy Spirit into their lives, I would probably have mumbled something about saying prayers and receiving Communion.

But wait a minute, you'll be saying. Surely you can't mean that! You couldn't have been a Christian all those years, and a priest of the Church of England, without knowing *something* of the Holy Spirit?

Maybe I am exaggerating – a little. But that's what it seemed like at the time. For in 1964 I became involved in the charismatic movement which was beginning to sweep through the Church. One day in the spring of that year, when I was praying alone, I was caught up in an inward joy and praised God in an unknown language. In the spirituality of the Pentecostal tradition, I was baptised in the Holy Spirit.[1]

Looking back, I reckon that the staleness and cynicism of previous years had masked a longing to find more of God in my life. Deep down I wanted him to rise up and take control of me. I could see how ineffective my ministry as a priest was, how lukewarm I was as a disciple of Christ. I wanted the faith that I had learned from childhood to leap into action.

And that's what seemed to happen. From then on I prayed with a new expectancy. I read the Bible with a new eagerness. I preached with a new authority. I had a new hope that, despite my weaknesses and limitations, God might still speak and act through me in my dealings with people. And I tried to allow a little more of his love to come into my relationships with them.

For me it was a fulfilment of Christ's promise, 'If anyone thirst, let him come to me and drink. He who believes in me, as the scripture has said, "Out of his heart shall flow rivers of living water"' (John 7: 37–8).

'You've changed!' said a member of the congregation a few months later. The tone in her voice implied that she thought the change might be for the better, but she wasn't sure!

The symbolism of water is evocative. When we first learn to swim, we put on armbands and gradually gain confidence to strike out with arms and legs. Then we take one armband off and strike out again, eventually daring to let our feet lift off the floor of the pool. Eventually we leave the remaining armband behind and discover, to our astonishment, that our bodies really are buoyant and that we can swim and dive.

Similarly with our spiritual growth. To begin with, the Lord provides us with families and congregations as encouragers to faith. Then he leads us to depend more on his strength and less on our own until circumstances offer us the opportunity of risking more of our lives to him. What is called baptism in the Holy Spirit can be one of the results of taking such risks.

Charismatics are sometimes accused of being so taken up with the Spirit and his gifts that they forget God the Father and overlook the centrality of Jesus Christ and his cross. All I can say in reply to that criticism is that I don't think I did. On the contrary, after my experience I came to appreciate all the more God's creative and redeeming work.

I would say, in fact, that my concept of God became more scriptural and more trinitarian. It became more scriptural because what the Bible reveals of the nature of God became more relevant to my experience of him in prayer, in the ministry and fellowship of the Church, and in the world as made by him. It became more trinitarian because the Holy Spirit was more real to me alongside my earlier understanding of God as Father and as incarnate Lord.

Belief in the Holy Spirit released me into a greater hope that God is One who speaks and acts now among us. Contemporary theological debates, which so often seem to suggest that God is powerless in his heaven with no means of intervening in the affairs of men and women, shrank in significance as I saw God at work in his Church and in his world, healing and transforming people, liberating them from dishabilitating situations, and equipping them with astonishing abilities.

It wasn't a question of coming to believe in miracles. It was a matter of recognising that the Lord works with us and shows that his Word is true.

Elisha's servant rose early in the morning and saw the Syrian army encircling the city. He ran to Elisha to raise the alarm. Then the prophet prayed, 'O Lord, open his eyes that he may see.' And the servant saw round his master horses and chariots of fire (2 Kings 6: 17). So the Holy Spirit enlightens us to see the realities of God which are hidden to our unhopeful and untrusting eyes.

One consequence was that my understanding of how God worked was turned upside-down. Previously I had tended to assume that Christian ministry was a partnership between God and myself – with God, of course, as the senior partner! Now I saw that, on such an assumption, I just got in God's way. Being more aware of the initiative of the Spirit, I realised that every ministry is *his* ministry, from start to finish, and that my role is to listen to his voice and to obey him. His thoughts are not my thoughts, neither are his ways my ways.

As my concept of God was being enlarged, so was my concept of the Church. Its spiritual and liturgical traditions vibrated with a fresh relevance. The writings of men and women of God and the prayers of the past came alive as I recognised in them the response to the Father through Jesus Christ by the Holy Spirit that I wanted to make, too. Sometimes you read a poem or listen to a piece of music and it so matches your mood that you're almost moved to tears by it. That's what began to happen to me as I dipped into the Church's spiritual and liturgical treasures.

Then my sense of *being* the Church deepened. It's easy to talk about the people of God and to quote the right scriptural texts and yet to miss the inner conviction that the Church is one through the anointing of the Holy Spirit. I now began to see the Church less in organisational terms and more in terms of a relationship between those who are baptised in the name of Jesus Christ. In other words, what mattered was what God was doing among people, not the details of their doctrines or their practices.

This affected two attitudes in me. First, it changed my attitude towards the so-called 'clergy line'. My training as a priest in the Anglican Church and my understanding of what ordination meant gave me a sense of being distanced from lay members of the congregation. (I might add that this sense of being distanced from them was reinforced by the tendency of some Anglicans to regard their clergy as strange creatures from outer space!)

Now I saw myself as one with them in sharing in the redemption of Christ and answering to the call of God by the power of his Spirit. By the one Spirit we exercised different gifts in a corporate ministry. When I stood in front of the congregation on Sunday mornings and gave the liturgical greeting, 'The Lord be with you,' their response, 'And also with you,' signified that together we were committing ourselves to follow the Spirit's leading in our common discipleship.

Second, it changed my attitude towards Christians of other denominations. I no longer wanted them to become Anglicans, preferably of an Anglo-Catholic variety. I saw denominational differences partly as an example of the different gifts of the Spirit and partly as a reminder that we were all still seeking the truth of the Gospel. I was less bothered whether or not a Free Church minister was episcopally ordained; I was more prepared to accept what the Lord ministered to me through him (or her).

No doubt these changes in my attitudes were influenced by the trends towards a fuller lay ministry and a greater ecumenical fellowship in the denominations in the 'sixties. But my involvement in the charismatic movement prepared me to appreciate these trends and give me the inner conviction that they were of God. Through them my ministry as a parish priest was considerably enriched.

Eventually I felt led to leave Romford and to join some friends who were forming a new community, the Barnabas Fellowship, at Whatcombe House in Dorset. There I experienced what it means to be the people of God in an intimate, family-like grouping. There I also experienced what Christian unity means when we are committed to disciples whose backgrounds varied from Roman Catholic to fundamentalist Evangelical.

Living, praying and working together in a common life-style was both a testing and a strengthening. Exposure to that kind of community living soon exposes our weaknesses (to others if not always to ourselves!). But it also discerns and encourages our spiritual gifts. My four years at Whatcombe enabled me to observe and share in the charismatic renewal as it touched individuals, groups and congregations in Britain and elsewhere. So much of my previous experience found a fulfilment in the corporate ministry of the community.[2]

And yet at no stage is our discipleship an end in itself. The Christian pilgrimage really is a going onward with the Holy Spirit to the next part of the journey. One stage prepares us for the next – with the Spirit's surprises. I had not expected to be married – yet the family life of the community prepared me to be a husband and a father in my own family. I had not expected to be called to an ecumenical ministry – and yet the ecumenical membership of the community prepared me for that kind of work in Manchester.

The purposes of God in our lives are unfolded one by one, like the pages of a good book. We are absorbed by what we're reading on the page in front of us, but we're also aware that the next page is going to be better still.

My experience teaches me that there is a continuity in God's dealings with us. We may be tempted to think that some new experience is our first real encounter with him. I know that at each of the steps of my own pilgrimage – such as it is up to the present – I've been tempted to look at it in that way. Just after my involvement with the charismatic renewal I thought I was taking Christian discipleship seriously for the first time, and after I joined the Barnabas Fellowship I thought I was becoming more committed to the Church. Because our Christian faith suddenly becomes more demanding, we tend to assume that everything we've experienced before was either phoney or second-class.

But I soon came to realise that such assumptions are dishonouring to God. God is at work in our lives long, long before we are aware of him. 'Before I formed you in the womb, I knew you, and before you were born I consecrated you' (Jer. 1: 5). God's word to his prophet is his word to us as well. His hand has been upon us from the moment when the first cells stirred in our mother's womb to commence the creation of a new human being. His hand remains on us still.

Every new coming of the Spirit into our lives invigorates and deepens every previous coming. All spiritual progress is in being drawn closer to God through Jesus Christ by the Holy Spirit. Earlier steps in that progress are not invalidated because they seem less significant compared with what we have experienced more recently.

Furthermore, to make absolute any one experience of the Spirit and to claim that it is real in a way other experiences weren't real is to run the risk of belittling the Lord rather than magnifying him. If we look at our past with thankfulness to him instead of with criticism of ourselves (and others), we shall see that past in a new light. We shall see that he is bringing alive *what he has already given us.*

Why, then, am I a Christian?

Answer: I'm a Christian because of God's loving choice and call.

That choice was made when he sent his Son Jesus Christ into the world to redeem us. That call was made when he forgave us and adopted us into his family through Jesus Christ by the Holy Spirit.

All that remains for us to do is to surrender to that choice and that call.

Initially it seems as if we're searching for him. With my whole heart I seek thee;' said the psalmist (Ps. 119: 10). Then we realise that in reality the Good Shepherd is searching for us. All God needs from us is the desire to be found by him with his forgiveness, his healing, his guidance, his strength-

---

[1] In *Greater Things than These* (Faith Press, 1974) I said that my involvement in the charismatic movement began in 1963. I made no note of it at the time and did not write about it until ten years later. Peter Hocken, who is doing some research into the origins of the movement, has evidence to show that my memory was faulty, and I am grateful to him for enabling me to correct the record.

[2] I have described this in *The Beginnings at Whatcombe* (Hodder and Stoughton, 1976).

ening, his joy. Life takes on a new character; it becomes one season of grace followed by another.

But to respond to God with our whole heart we need to be orientated towards his Holy Spirit. What this implies we shall discuss in the next chapter.

CHAPTER 2

The Breath of God

The Orient, a name for the East, is derived from the Latin, *oriens*, meaning the sunrise. Church buildings which are planned so that their chancels point towards the East are said to be orientated. Orientation is an in-built faculty in humans and animals that enables them to find their way home, like the birds which travel over long distances to return to their nests. The word can also mean a course held in a college to assist freshers to find their way around.

To be orientated towards the Holy Spirit, then, is to live in such a manner that he directs every step of our journey. It is like setting out across the desert with the determination to walk towards the point where the sun rises without being deflected to the right or left. Orientation towards the Holy Spirit means that we constantly have to check what our aim in life is and what we have to do each day to be faithful to that aim.

Before we can follow the Spirit, we have to listen to him, and that means giving him the whole of our attention. This is another aspect of orientation. When I am in the company of a child, I have to adjust myself to his capacities and needs. I must use language he can understand, join the games he can play, walk at a pace he can manage, and so on. In other words I conduct myself in an attitude of complete awareness of his presence.

Similarly with the Spirit. Unless I live in the awareness of his presence, and relate what I say and do to his will and his power, I shall soon be cutting myself off from his influence. I shall be going my own way instead of God's way.

Let us summarise the scriptural teaching on the Holy Spirit's role in the work of our salvation to see why this orientation is so necessary – fundamental, in fact, to our Christian discipleship.

In coming to redeem us, God finds us human beings in a shattered, disorientated condition. The disintegration of our personalities and the loss of self-control are but two aspects of our sinful and fallen condition. His gracious purpose is to bring us into a reconciled relationship with himself through Jesus Christ and, in the outworking of that relationship, to reintegrate us and to reorientate us and so make us the kind of people he destines us to be.

That relationship with God is restored by Jesus Christ through the sacrifice on Calvary. Paul expounded this mystery in terms of an exchange: 'For our sake he [God] made him [Christ] to be sin who knew no sin, so that in him we might become the righteousness of God' (2 Cor. 5: 21). Paul did not say that Christ became a sinner, for that would not have been true; nor did he say that every believer immediately and automatically becomes righteous, as good as God, for that would certainly not have been true, either. He said that Christ became sin, that is, Jesus came to stand where sinful man stands, estranged from God, so that through his cross and resurrection we are able to stand where he stands, in a relationship of union with God. Thus set right with God ('made righteous' or 'justified') and adopted into God's family through repentance, faith and baptism, we are now in his care. Nothing can separate us from the love of God in Christ (Rom. 8: 32–9).

But the task of reintegrating us and reorientating us so that we are made into the kind of people God destines us to be is a life-long process of growth and transformation. Sanctification – the purifying and strengthening work of God in our minds, attitudes, values, emotions and relationships with others – continues until we die. It will not be completed until 'the redemption of our bodies' (Rom. 8:

23). Even the depths of our unconscious, where hidden fears and depressions lurk, will need to be cleansed and liberated for the final union of ourselves with God in Christ.

This work of sanctification is particularly the operation of the Third Person of the Trinity – 'God closer than close', as I heard him described in a sermon recently. The Spirit is God active in the deepest intimacy possible within everything that makes us the people we are. He is doing a thorough renovation job.

Years ago I saw the Genesis 2 account of the creation of man beautifully depicted on a film. The camera had been trained on a wide stretch of sand. All was still until a breath of wind stirred the surface of the sand with tiny ripples. Then the ripples grew larger until grooves and little heaps began to form. As the wind became stronger, the grooves and little heaps ran together to make the faint outline of a man lying on his back. It was like the rough shaping of a stone after the sculptor has finished the preliminary stage of his task. The wind gusted until the details of the body emerged – face, trunk, arms, legs and feet. At last, when the figure of the actor was completely exposed, he stirred, raised himself up, and slowly stood up naked in the sunlight.

To be orientated towards the Spirit is to surrender ourselves to the redeeming love of God so that his breath can re-create us in every corner of our humanity. Then we shall be mentally, psychologically and spiritually whole, as well as physically complete, reflecting the glory of God himself.

Until this state of bliss is reached – and we affirm our faith in God's destiny for us as human beings when we say in the Creed, 'I believe in the resurrection of the body' – we shall be inwardly divided between God's will and ours, between good and evil. Sin dwells in us, defeated but not yet destroyed. The battle won on the cross has to be appropriated in our daily lives. This is our spiritual warfare.

The theme is persistent in Christian spirituality. Its origins are in the Old Testament, especially the psalms, where petitions for deliverance from enemies were interpreted as prayers for protection from the spiritual forces that assail us. 'He reached from on high, he took me, he drew me out of many waters' (Ps. 18: 16). That psalm may well have referred at one time to David's defeat of the Philistines, as 2 Samuel 22 suggests; but in Israel's worship and then in the Church's it was applied to the saving work of God in rescuing his people from sin.

Accounts of Old Testament campaigns are seen as allegories of our spiritual warfare. When David confronted the Philistine champion with his sling, he ended his challenge with the words, 'the battle is the Lord's, and he will give you into our hand' (1 Sam. 17: 47). Similarly, when the men of Judah were gathered in preparation for the attack on Moab and Ammon, we are told that, 'the Spirit of the Lord came upon Jahaziel... And he said, "Thus says the Lord to you, 'Fear not, and be not dismayed at this great multitude; for the battle is not yours but God's'"' (2 Chr. 20: 14–15). Such words have encouraged countless Christians as they have sought God's grace to aid them in personal difficulties.

The evangelists discerned the signs of that warfare in the ministry of Jesus. The temptations in the wilderness were the opening skirmishes; the climax came in the Garden of Gethsemane. The theme is taken up in the epistles where the apostolic authors exhorted their readers to endure the trials and tests that would come upon them.

But Paul went further. More than any other New Testament writer he analysed the nature of the struggle which we experience, in order to encourage his readers to rely utterly upon the power of God's Spirit.

His understanding of our human nature – his psychological framework – was this. Our human nature is composed of flesh, soul and spirit. *Soul* is the faculty of life itself, that which makes us living beings. *Spirit* denotes those higher or moral qualities which strive to govern our conduct, that part of ourselves which responds to God enabling us to understand his Word and to know his will. *Flesh* is not just our physical make-up; it is ourselves as prone to be governed by the desires and impulses of our fallen nature with its appetites and fears. With this framework Paul explained why, although we are created by God, we have an in-built weakness which tends to alienate us from God when we are faced with the choice of obeying or rejecting him. Our spirit might be willing but our flesh is weak.

Into this human nature God comes in strength by his Spirit. Poured out on us, his Spirit fills our spirits and his divine power flows into our lives. Openness to the Spirit, then, is vital if we are to be his disciples. Therefore, said the apostle, you must be led by the Spirit, let the Spirit rule your hearts, do not quench the Spirit, do not grieve the Spirit, endeavour to guard the unity of the Spirit in the bond of peace. It is through the Spirit that we are being changed from one degree of glory to another as we are drawn by him nearer to God through Jesus Christ.

Now it is a matter of experience that, although we think of Christian discipleship as a steady pilgrimage, spiritual growth seems to happen episodically – in fits and starts, to put it crudely. Crisis points in our lives often play an important part. Confronted with a need for God, we take the risk of throwing ourselves on his mercy and grace more than we have done before, to discover that the everlasting arms are beneath us in situations where we had not expected to find them.

Looking back later on these crisis points, we see that they were the beginnings of fresh seasons of grace in our lives. That, I believe, is how the Pentecostal baptism in the Holy Spirit is best understood.

I will illustrate this by quoting from two letters which I received recently.[1]

The first letter came from a mother in her mid-thirties who described herself as having been brought up 'within the Church of England system'. She had been confirmed as a teenager and attended church more or less regularly since.

Her children were baptised as babies and she contributed actively in parochial life out of a strong sense of responsibility. 'There have been times when being a Christian and church-going made more sense than others,' she wrote.

About a year before she wrote the letter she had gone to the doctor for anti-depressants, but after a time – with his agreement – gave them up and received the laying-on of hands for healing in her church. She felt more able to cope with life, but also became more aware of how superficial her faith was. She continued:

Then two significant events took place. First, I attended an evening of prayer and praise in another church; and although I was not entirely at ease when I first went, I returned on other occasions. Second, I went to an open service on healing and plucked up courage to ask to be filled with the Holy Spirit.

For two weeks everything was marvellous. God loved me! Church services really did mean what they said. Prayer and praise came naturally. Everything worked! But soon the nagging doubts started up again. Life wasn't like that! Just look round at the world outside. I had indulged in a religious experience and not in reality – or had I?

Difficult months followed. She found herself driven by an insatiable quest for the things of God, reading book after book. She tried to be more disciplined about her prayers – and failed. Eventually she asked God for the gift of tongues and started stammering a few strange words.

Day-to-day living was still a struggle. I needed to take tablets from time to time although I desperately wanted not to. Christmas came and went amid mixed emotions. A lot of pieces now fitted together much better than in the past and I could keep up a pretty good front. But where, oh where, were joy and peace?

Eventually I found them, and the thought of taking any more tablets went out of the window. A new study group was forming in our parish and, although I badly wanted to be part of it, I felt that other members of the group knew more of the answers than I did. The first meetings seemed to confirm my suspicions. I appeared to be very much at variance with the general consensus of opinion. I had to apologise to a person on whom I had been trying to work out my frustrations.

I realised there had been too much of 'I' in my life. A light slowly began to appear. I owed everything to God. I could do nothing without him. It was time to trust him completely. Within a few weeks I was asked to lead the prayer group. During the meeting someone gave thanks for me and prayed that I should know joy and peace. The next day I did. Of course, it did not end there. Life flows on.

The second letter came from a man of about the same age:

It was about three o'clock in the morning when I put down the receiver after yet another long telephone conversation with the Samaritans. I had been thinking, not just about suicide, but about what would be the best way to set about it. I did not have enough courage even though my world had fallen to pieces: I had lost my job; my marriage was on the rocks; I was weak and in pain following an operation some months before; I had financial problems; I was estranged from family and friends; on tranquillisers, depressed and unable to cope with simple tasks. Hamlet's words came back to me time and time again: 'O! . . . that the Everlasting had not fixed his canon 'gainst self-slaughter! O God! O God! How weary, stale, flat and unprofitable seem to me all the uses of this world.' And again I had phoned the Samaritans in despair.

He had had some contact with the Church and received Communion occasionally, so at last he went to see a vicar he knew who lived near by. A long interview followed. Eventually he cried out, 'I want to be made whole!' and fell on his knees, confessing his sins. The vicar prayed for him and laid hands on his head as he pronounced the absolution.

On the vicar's advice, he went to talk to a Roman Catholic priest, experienced in the ministry of prayer counselling, who helped him to recognise the bitterness and resentment that had piled up in him during the course of his life. He left, freed of a great burden and realising how far he had allowed his feelings to keep him away from God.

A day or two later I found myself at a healing service in a little church about a dozen miles away. There were about ten people present and I wondered what on earth I was doing there. After some friendly chat one with another, the vicar led us into a time of prayer, thanksgiving and praise, and then invited any who needed healing to ask for it. The exact opposite of what I expected now happened. As I began to ask for healing, one of the others near me knelt down, and I felt myself impelled to join those gathered round in the laying-on of hands.

For the first time in my life I became aware of the physical presence of the Holy Spirit. It was as if the Spirit was flowing through me and down my arms and hands into the kneeling figure before me.

What was happening to me? I am still finding out, and I expect to go on discovering the answer for the rest of my life. To me, 'conversion' is nearly, but not quite, the right expression, as I had reserved it for the heathen and non-believer. 'Baptism in the Spirit' I tend to reserve for people who undergo a single and definite experience. And yet, over the course of a few days, a tremendous change had taken place in my life. I was surrounded by the warmth, love, friendship and support of churchgoers. I now had an identity. I was a member of the body of Christ.

There isn't room to write at length about all the wonderful things that are now happening in my life. My physical strength has returned, my financial problems resolved, relationships with my family and friends are being healed, and no more drugs. Prayers are always answered, sometimes at once, sometimes over a period of time. I find joy in Christian fellowship and seek opportunities to witness. God speaks to me as a friend through the Bible and is using me to work his purpose out. He is with me day and night: healing, removing worry, solving problems, supporting, giving strength and achieving where I alone can do nothing.

I no longer need to telephone those wonderful people, the Samaritans. God is on the line all the time.

What the writers of these letters each experienced was the new life of the risen Christ breaking through into their lives. Using the terminology of Paul's psychological framework, they found the Holy Spirit pouring into their spirits, souls and bodies. They were learning something of what it means to be transferred from the present age to the age which is to come; they were becoming 'a new creation' (2 Cor. 5: 17).

To return to the two letters. Although from different people about different experiences, there is a basic similarity between them.

1. Both writers had reached a crisis point in their lives. For the man it was a desperate one, for he had become suicidal. The woman found her comfortable domestic existence threatened by depression.

2. Both had some links with the Church and knew something of faith in Jesus Christ. But neither the links or the faith seemed to have been very strong. For the woman it was a matter of social responsibility: 'There have been times when being a Christian and church-going made more sense than others.' For the man it was little more than a casual interest.

3. In the crises, both experienced a sense of unworthiness.

The woman realised how superficial her faith was and how much she needed God. The man came to see his life was in such a mess that he could only finish it or surrender it to God. I believe this was a sign of the Spirit: 'when he comes he will convince the world concerning sin and righteousness and judgment' (John 16: 8).

4. The next step was to take the risk of believing that God could heal them. The woman decided to do without the anti-depressants (though only after consulting her doctor: a wise precaution, for it is almost always dangerous to abandon medication in the hope that God will heal directly). The man's healing began when he poured out his woes to his vicar and received absolution and the laying-on of hands; it continued through the counselling of the Roman Catholic priest (a nice ecumenical touch, that).

5. Inner healing – or, as it is sometimes called, prayer counselling – was important in both cases. This is a ministry in which the 'client' discusses experiences from his past life that have troubled him in later years, and in which the 'minister' invokes the power of God to break the bondages those experiences still have over him. In the woman this was a lengthy struggle, perhaps because she was still fighting those bondages in her own strength rather than in surrendering to God. In the man the struggle was shorter.

6. Both sought a renewal or baptism in the Holy Spirit and, as a result, found themselves ministering to others. Despite her fears, the woman took the lead in a prayer group. The man laid hands on others for healing and became aware of himself as a ministering member of the body of Christ. Healings and spiritual renewal are not just to make life different for us – even if joyfully different. They are to equip us for God's purposes within the fellowship and mission of the Church.

Many Christians learn to become more orientated towards the Holy Spirit as a result of a crisis in their lives. Personal testimonies which have been told in the current charismatic movement illustrate this again and again, like the two letters I have quoted.

But we do not *have* to wait for a crisis in our own lives before we do anything ourselves! We can turn to God on any day and ask him to renew our discipleship of his Son through the in-filling of the Holy Spirit.

There are certain steps we have to take – steps which I will now list. We can take these steps in prayer alone, although it is often helpful to ask others to pray with us through at least some of them.

The first step is to make an act of penitence. We review our lives, asking the Holy Spirit to reveal sins that we have not discerned and blockages which prevent us from receiving his cleansing in areas of our personalities. God knows everything about us, and why we are what we are. 'I the Lord search the mind and try the heart, to give to every man according to his ways, according to the fruit of his doings' (Jer. 17: 10). We need to see ourselves as he sees us. Our experience of living and working with others, outside as well as inside the Christian community, will help us to move towards this perspective. Then we shall know what to confess.

Included in an act of penitence is a renunciation of evil. In our society we lay ourselves open to evil influences in all kinds of ways – not just the immoral, deceitful and blasphemous influences that come into our homes through the media, but also practices such as the occult, spiritualism and fortune-telling.

Before we can confess our sins, we sometimes have to be liberated from resentments and anxieties that haunt us from the past – half-hidden and persistent, either because we don't know how to be freed from them, or because in a perverse manner we have secretly cherished them as part of our make-up. Counselling may be necessary to help us face them and pray for God's forgiveness and inner healing.

The next step is to make an act of faith. Even if we have done this often before, it is still necessary to affirm that we are turning once more away from ourselves towards Jesus Christ. Paul was addressing Christians who had already received Christ into their lives and known the first fruits of the Spirit (Rom. 8: 23) when he urged them, 'Because of God's great mercy to us I appeal to you: offer yourselves as a living sacrifice to God, dedicated to his service and pleasing to him. This is the true worship that you should offer' (Rom. 12: 1 TEV).

This act of faith is crucial. Yet it is precisely here we tend to hesitate. We know that, if we make it, it means less self-love, self-indulgence, self-satisfaction. Offering ourselves as a living sacrifice to God means the death of self. As Christ died on the cross, so our self-centredness also has to die. Only in this way can the renewal of our minds and wills continue.

Not all intellectual problems will be solved. We shall have doubts, we shall have questions. But submission to the Word of God, and particularly submission to his Word brought to us in the Bible, will enable us to receive God's grace through the doubts and the questions. They will not disappear, but they will be seen in the perspective of following God's Word and trusting that in him all will one day be revealed.

Similarly, by submitting our wills to God, and especially those emotions which dominate or deflect us, we shall gradually learn how to discern God's guidance in any situation in which we find ourselves. We shall not be infallible, we shall make mistakes. But, by being more orientated towards the Holy Spirit, we shall become aware of the way in which he wants us to go.

The third step is to ask God to send the Holy Spirit into our lives through the saving work of Jesus Christ. At the end of his teaching on prayer Jesus said, 'If you then, who are evil, know how to give good gifts to your children, how much more will the heavenly Father give the Holy Spirit to those who ask him!' (Luke 11: 13). If an earthly father, with all his faults and follies, provides for the needs of his children, the heavenly Father in the perfection of his love can be relied on to give the best possible gift of all – himself in Spirit – to those who ask.

Formally this is done in the liturgy at those moments in our lives when we move to the next important stage in our pilgrimage – when we are confirmed, married, anointed for healing, or commissioned to an office or particular mission in the local church.

Informally this is done when we invite a group of Christians to pray for us with the laying-on of hands. Having gone through the previous two steps privately or with a counsellor or confessor, we sit or kneel, relaxed but expectant, inwardly committing ourselves to God. Around us our friends are praying aloud in English or in tongues.

Perhaps they say something like this:

'Heavenly Father, your Son Jesus Christ told us that you give good gifts to your children who ask in faith. Thank you for all that you have given your child through baptism and life in the Church until now. Thank you for the signs of your mercy and grace in the past. Now fill your servant afresh with your Holy Spirit, that (s)he may be a more faithful disciple of your Son. Grant him (her) those gifts that will enable him (her) to serve you in company with your people in your world to the glory of your holy name.'

Perhaps one of our friends has an inspired word from the Lord for us. We make a mental note of it, intending to test it later. Another quotes a passage, a scripture. Maybe another has a picture which reveals something of God's will to us.

Then we pray aloud ourselves, in English or in tongues; if the latter, there may be an interpretation, which also has to be tested. We know an inner peace. There is a silence. We end with an act of thanksgiving and praise to God.

We may feel elated. That's a blessing to thank God for, but we must not slip into the trap of believing experiences of the Holy Spirit are primarily to do with how we feel. Living by the Spirit has to do with the whole of our lives, when we're feeling fed up and depressed as well as when we're feeling happy and fulfilled. Let's enjoy the sense of being given God's grace through the prayers of our friends, but let's also look for something much deeper to happen in us as well.

We may exercise a new spiritual gift, like speaking in tongues. Again, that's a blessing, too, but we must not regard the manifestation as a sign of instant personal sanctity. The New Testament warns us about counterfeits. And, in any case, God can choose to work through us on a particular occasion whether or not we happen to be obedient to him. He can effect his will through whom he chooses, even using those who oppose him, like the scribes and Pharisees.

The only true sign of the Spirit's work in our lives is when others see Jesus Christ reflected more clearly through us. It is what we are as persons, and especially what we are in our relationships with others, that affirms the reality of the Spirit's presence in our lives – or denies that presence.

Paul called this sign 'the fruit of the Spirit' (Gal. 5: 22). The singular form of the noun, 'fruit' not 'fruits', is noteworthy. The fruit stem from one source from which they flow – the Lord himself. The image is close to that of the vine in John 15, where Jesus claimed the fulfilment of the Old Testament prophecies of the vine of Israel. The disciples, as branches, are to abide in Christ as he abides in them, and then they will bear fruit (vv. 4–5).

The abiding presence of God the Holy Spirit in our lives is the means by which we mature as disciples of Jesus Christ and become fruitful for the Father's purposes.

Love is listed as the first of the Spirit's fruit, not only because it is pre-eminent but also because it embraces all the rest. Joy is second because it is the produce of love, 'the blush of love', as someone once described it. Peace is the Easter *shalom* of the risen Christ, a quality in the individual and in the Christian community which is instantly recognised. With the other fruit listed by the apostle, such virtues are a foretaste of the kingdom of God.

'For the kingdom of God ... is righteousness and peace and joy in the Holy Spirit' (Rom. 14: 17). The same note is sounded in the famous hymn of love in 1 Corinthians 13. But what makes this regime possible is that those who are committed to Jesus Christ as their Lord and Saviour have 'crucified the flesh with its passions and desires' (Gal. 5: 24). That is what we are about when we ask God to send his Holy Spirit.

So we usually have to ask friends to pray with us on a number of occasions – at the beginning of a new phase in our lives, in taking counsel towards an important decision, in moments of crisis. Although I can date my baptism in the Spirit experience to a day in 1964, there have been times since when I have invited others to lay hands on me and ask God to renew me again in his Spirit.

Then, having done that, we believe the Holy Spirit has come to us and act in that belief. Whether we feel anything or not, living by the Spirit is ultimately a matter of faith. We only become aware of his presence as we go about the business of daily living with that attitude of mind and will.

'Let me ask you only this,' said Paul: 'Did you receive the Spirit by works of the law, or by hearing with faith?' (Gal. 3: 2).

There's no doubt what answer he expected.

[1] Copies of these letters were sent to me for comment by the editors of the *Oxford Diocesan Magazine* (May 1983), and I am grateful for their permission to use them here.

CHAPTER 3

The Rhythm of Life

Right! you say. I understand I must be more orientated towards the Holy Spirit if I am to be a disciple of Jesus Christ. I must submit to the Spirit, ask him to fill me, believe I'm receiving him, and endeavour to be more obedient to him.

But what then? Where do I begin to do this in the practical business of everyday living? How do I start?

At this point some Christians are liable to be afflicted with the 'if only' syndrome. If only I'd married a Christian, if only I went to a more supportive church, if only I was in a less exacting job, if only I'd brought my kids up differently – the variations of the complaint are endless.

The disease is aggravated when we make comparisons. There's always someone in the congregation who is more advantageously placed than we are! Stories of individual Christians, read in books or recounted at meetings, make us feel unspiritual weaklings.

The corrective to the 'if only' syndrome is the truth that being a disciple of Jesus Christ is not a competitive business. It may be like entering a race, but it's the kind of race in which all can win prizes (1 Cor. 9: 24). We drop out of the running when we become discontented or jealous.

When Peter asked the risen Christ what was to be the destiny of the beloved disciple, the Lord replied, 'If it is my will that he remain until I come, what is that to you? Follow me!' (John 21: 23). In other words, keep your eyes on Christ, not on other followers! If it is God's will that one disciple should do something extraordinary (that seems to be the implication of Christ's words, 'that he remain until I come'), then others should pray that the disciple in question will be enabled to fulfil that ministry. The same lesson underlies the parable of the labourers in the vineyard (Matt. 20: 1–16).

The word disciple, as everyone knows, means 'one who follows'. Succeeding generations of Christians have understood that to be a disciple of Jesus Christ means going on an inner and spiritual journey, renouncing the past and entering into his new way of living in the present and in the future. But that journey is undertaken in life as we know it now.

In Corinth there were some who wanted to leave unbelieving husbands because they thought they could be better disciples if they did. In Thessalonia there were some who regarded their daily work as unnecessary if the Lord was to return quickly. Paul's reply was the rule that he had laid down in all the churches he had founded: 'Each one should go on living according to the Lord's gift to him, and as he was when he called him' (1 Cor. 7: 17 TEV).

We have to learn to be disciples of Jesus Christ where we are. It is true that some have to make radical changes. The call to be a disciple in full-time Christian work or in a religious community means a different life. Those who are in jobs or situations which contradict their Christian witness have to resign or move on, trusting the Lord to provide for them in other ways. But for most of us following Christ has to be fulfilled in the midst of our everyday life at home, at work and at leisure.

What we do each day usually happens within a regular rhythm. From when we wake up until when we fall asleep, we are caught up in a cycle of events and meetings which usually follow a similar pattern each day. We get out of bed, wash, dress, have breakfast; take the children to school, drive, ride or walk to the office, shop or whatever; do our morning jobs, have coffee-breaks, lunch-breaks and tea-breaks, and so on. Those who spend more time at home –

housewives, unemployed, disabled, invalids, retired, elderly – also have their pattern of daily activities.

At weekends the rhythm changes. Saturdays and Sundays have their own programmes – shopping, gardening, church-going, social occasions, sporting interests. So do the seasons and the years. In families with younger members at school or college, term-time and vacation-time have characteristics of their own which affect the pattern of life for the whole household. And the rhythm changes as we move from childhood to adolescence, from single to married life, from working life to redundancy or retirement.

The rhythm of life is often determined by others – those we live and work and associate with. At work what we do is dictated by the job and our responsibilities to employers and fellow-employees. At home the need to look after husband, wife, children, parents, friends, and casual callers affects the way we spend our time. Those who care for the very young, the sick, and the elderly are involved in a round of washing, feeding, administering medicine and tidying up.

To be a disciple within these rhythms of life, it is necessary to make a space for prayer in each day. Once we have allocated such a space in our time-table, we shall gradually form a habit which – even if it doesn't guarantee real prayer – will make prayer more likely. (Answering the objection that habits are hardly worthy of the Lord, a priest I knew said, 'There's nothing wrong with a habit if it's a good one!')

By creating space for prayer in our lives each day, we shall show we mean business with God. If we don't, we shall be in danger of pushing him to the margin of our concerns instead of inviting him to be the centre of them. Casualness in prayer leads to casualness in Christian living.

I know there are some who will find this extremely difficult, if not impossible, at some periods of their lives – the man who has to take drugs and finds all his energy sapped struggling to keep his job, the young mother exhausted by the demands of a sick baby, the invalid whose mind is blurred with pain. But even if we can only offer the briefest arrow prayers at set moments during the day, that is still real prayer.

'That's beyond me,' said one woman, after hearing a sermon on daily prayer. 'My mind is so sluggish when I get up, it's as much as I can do to get to work in the morning.'

She was having psychiatric treatment and took tranquillisers at night.

Her listener, another woman in the congregation, knew this and said, 'Why don't you be like a little child who runs to its mother in the morning and cries, "Mummy, give me a hug for today"?'

The first woman looked at her thoughtfully.

'Thank you for saying that,' she said. 'I'll do it.'

How long should we pray?

I keep what Jack Winslow used to call 'the morning watch' and allocate a set time for it when I get up. I look at the clock to make sure I don't shorten it. If for any reason I fail to do this, I try to make up for it later in the day (usually without much success!). I also pray for a shorter time before going to bed.

The length of time is a personal matter. It's usually better to begin with a realistic period and gradually lengthen it as you go on. A guide could be the length of time you would want to spend with a best friend each day in order to keep in close touch.

Where can we pray?

A friend of mine who works in London uses his long journey on the Underground. He joins the train at the beginning of its route, so he is always able to secure the same corner seat in a carriage. He reads his Bible and prays while everyone around him is immersed in the morning papers.

A woman who takes her dog for a walk over some fields every morning sings choruses aloud from the moment she steps over the stile to the moment she returns to it. Commuters use city churches during their lunch hour.

A girl who was converted when she was 18 began praying at home after tea. But her mother was so antagonised by the sight of her daughter reading the Bible that the girl retreated to the bathroom to pray while the rest of the family were watching TV.

'They're used to my being in there a long time,' she explained with a wistful smile.

And what shall we do when we pray?

For the rest of this chapter I want to draw out two lessons concerning prayer, which will help us to use the space we create for it fruitfully. One lesson is from the New Testament; the other is from the worship of the Church.

The first is focused on Jesus' own teaching about prayer.

When his disciples asked him to teach them to pray, he did not give a list of instructions about prayer techniques. He simply invited them to share in his own prayer to the Father: 'Our Father.' Since we are sons and daughters of God by adoption through the saving work of Jesus Christ, we can join him in his prayer. The same Spirit who brings us the freedom of God makes it possible to be united with Christ's prayer.

The movement of prayer – if I may call it that – is from Jesus to the Father in the Holy Spirit. It is an expression of the eternal love within the mystery of God the Holy Trinity. Our prayer becomes a reality when we allow the Spirit to pray in us. That is why all Christian worship is 'in the Spirit'.

Prayer, then, is the turning of our whole attention to God and submitting to the Spirit as he directs our lives through Christ to the Father. The deepest longings of our hearts – longings which we are incapable of expressing or even being fully aware of – can become the raw material for prayer through the cleansing and illumination of the Spirit of God. 'Likewise the Spirit helps us in our weakness; for we do not know how to pray as we ought, but the Spirit himself intercedes for us with sighs too deep for words' (Rom. 8: 26).

This comes out strikingly in the salutation at the end of 2 Corinthians: 'The grace of the Lord Jesus Christ and the love of God and the fellowship of the Holy Spirit be with you all.'

The text has become so familiar to us (especially through the practice of repeating it in chorus at the end of services and prayer-meetings) that we are likely to miss its profound meaning.

The grace of the Lord Jesus Christ is an observable event in human history. That grace is freely offered in Christ to us and to men and women of all time. Behind that grace, manifested in the life, death and resurrection of Jesus, is *the love of God* which, shining through Christ, is an eternal fact. It is the essential nature of God's being to love. *The fellowship of (or, the participation in) the Holy Spirit* is not only the community created by the Spirit among those who recognise the love of God and need the grace of Christ. It is also the means through which we are introduced into the intimate company of God the Father through the Son.

The text contains a whole theology of prayer in condensed form. And it is the basis for a simple picture which I sometimes have when I settle down to try and pray. The picture may owe something to the illustrations in the family Bible I mentioned in the first chapter.

God dwells far above me in inaccessible light. Standing, kneeling or sitting below him, I am conscious of my humanity and its weaknesses – my thoughts, my feelings, my physical condition. I am also conscious of my utter separateness from him – a gulf so wide that nothing in me could ever hope to bridge it.

But God has not remained on his side of the gulf. In Christ he has come to me and shared my humanity – my thoughts, my feelings, my physical condition, everything except my sinfulness. And through his cross I have access, with all other disciples, to the throne of grace. My attempts to pray are signals to God that I want to come before him in Christ. My life contains the raw material of that prayer which has to be cleansed, redirected, reinforced and transfigured by his Spirit. Only then can I enter into praise, confession, intercession and thanksgiving. Only then do I become aware that the God who dwells in inaccessible light dwells in me, too.

Creating space for prayer in the daily rhythm of our lives is deliberately placing ourselves where the Holy Spirit can pray through us. It is true that the Spirit can and will move us to prayer at any time and in any place – more so as we become disciplined in discerning his promptings. But the setting aside of a pause in the day facilitates this. These minutes in our prayer-space are offered to God for him to use so that we may more clearly hear his Word and more obediently respond to him. Through those minutes all other minutes in the day may be consecrated to him.

Notice that Jesus taught his disciples to say, *our* Father. God is not *my* Father. My relationship with him is not an exclusive one. He is my Father because he is also your Father, and he is our Father because we are united by the Spirit in his Son. The practical implication of this is that when we are praying alone we are not alone. We are members of the body of Christ and joined in prayer by the one Spirit.

Some groups of Christians make a pact to pray at the same time each day. During the war there was a widespread movement to pray for peace when the chimes of Big Ben were heard over the radio each evening. The sense of fellowship in the Spirit which such a pact brings to those who participate in it is remarkable.

To pray, then, is to be caught up within the dynamic relationship of love which is at the heart of the Holy Trinity.

Before we move on to the second lesson concerning prayer from the worship of the Church, we can note that liturgical tradition has been faithful to this biblical pattern I have just been outlining.

Practically all formal prayers in the liturgy are addressed to God the Father; the Son and the Holy Spirit are referred to in the text of the prayer in relation to their role in the movement of prayer within the life of the Holy Trinity. Look

at almost any ancient collect and the biblical pattern is clear,
e.g.,

> Almighty God,
> without you we are not able to please you.
> Mercifully grant that your Holy Spirit
> may in all things direct and rule our hearts;
> through Jesus Christ our Lord.
>
> *Alternative Service Book*,
> Pentecost 6

The worship of the Church presents us with an ordered
pattern of daily prayer in what used to be known as 'the
divine office' (from the Latin *officium*, 'duty'); nowadays it
is given the beautiful and evocative name of 'the liturgy of
the hours'.

The custom of praying each day goes back beyond the
beginnings of Christianity to Judaism. Morning and
evening sacrifices were offered in the temple at Jerusalem.
Devout Jews observed times of prayer. The apostolic
congregation in Jerusalem attended the temple each day
(Acts 2: 46). Peter and John were on their way to pray at the
evening sacrifice when they met the crippled man (Acts 3: 1).
Peter was praying at midday on the roof-top of the house of
Simon the tanner in Joppa when he had a vision (Acts 10: 9),
and Paul and Silas went out to find a place of prayer when
they arrived in Philippi (Acts 16: 13).

During the centuries these customs crystallised into a
series of daily services which have come down to us in
varying forms, the most commonly known being Morning
and Evening Prayer in the *Prayer Book* and the *Alternative
Service Book*. In religious communities a fuller and more
varied liturgy of the hours is used.

Behind this long tradition we can discern the leading of
the Holy Spirit as he guided the people of God to offer their
daily prayers to the Father through Jesus Christ. The
ringing of church bells on weekdays and the radio

broadcasts of Evensong from cathedrals are reminders of that tradition. From the liturgy of the hours we can help ourselves to material and a framework for our daily prayers.

1. Different times of the day focus on different objectives in our discipleship.

Morning prayers remind us of the renewal of God's love that is symbolised in the sunrising.

> The steadfast love of the Lord never ceases,
>   his mercies never come to an end;
> they are new every morning;
>   great is thy faithfulness (Lam. 3: 22–3).

Because the new covenant was established through the death and resurrection of Christ on Easter morning, daybreak is a symbol of the power of that victory. To rise in the morning is to rise with Christ and to be equipped by the Spirit to serve him throughout that day. This interpretation of daybreak appears in one of the earliest of Christian hymns by Ambrose, Bishop of Milan (339–97), whose sermons were instrumental in the conversion of Augustine:

> O splendour of God's glory bright,
> Who bringest forth the light from Light;
> O Light, of light the fountain-spring;
> O Day, our days illumining;
>
> Come, very Sun of truth and love,
> Come in thy radiance from above,
> And shed the Holy Spirit's ray
> On all we think or do today.

Evening prayers, on the other hand, encourage us to reflect on the end of the age and the fulfilment of God's purposes in his kingdom. A canticle like the 'Nunc Dimittis' breathes a sense of thankfulness to God for all that he has done for us and looks forward to the time when his servant will know the divine rest:

Lord, now you let your servant go in peace:
   your word has been fulfilled.
My own eyes have seen the salvation:
   which you have prepared in the sight of every people;
a light to reveal you to the nations:
   and the glory of your people Israel.

2. The liturgy of the hours majors on praise. The opening versicle and response of Morning and Evening Prayer strike this note:

O Lord, open our lips;
   and our mouth shall proclaim your praise.

From earliest times the first psalm of the day has been the 'Venite':

O come, let us sing out to the Lord:
   let us shout in triumph to the rock of our salvation.

The psalms and the canticles are arranged so that praise continually returns to our prayers. On a cold, dark morning, when there's plenty to get depressed about, an act of praise brings the light and love of God into our lives.

A solicitor told me the other day that his secretary brings a cassette player into his office and they join in singing choruses while the mail is being sorted.

'I read my letters in a better spirit!' he said.

Praise draws our attention away from ourselves, our feelings and our problems, to God who rules our lives. Praising him for creating and redeeming us, we see our situation from the viewpoint of his purposes.

Some years ago there appeared a spate of books elaborating the Pauline injunction to praise God in all circumstances. They rightly emphasised that we should above all be a people who worship God in praise. But the idea got about that prayers of praise were like magic switches which could change any situation and convert tragedy into triumph.

That, of course, is a travesty of Paul's teaching. When he exhorted his readers to 'sing psalms and hymns and spiritual songs with thankfulness in your hearts to God' (Col. 3: 16), he was not telling them to delude themselves. He was saying that when we turn to God in praise and thankfulness, we are placing ourselves in an attitude of openness and dependence on him; he is then able to guide and equip us with his Spirit for all that we encounter.

3. The liturgy of the hours makes extensive use of the psalms. Initially Christians find the psalms strange, outlandish, and in a few places even repulsive. Then comes a moment when some of the psalms spring to life for us. They become relevant. They match our moods. They say things we feel we ought to say but can't find the right words ourselves. Gradually the psalter becomes a precious prayer-book.

The psalms represent God's Word which we can use in response to him. Originating in the experiences of the people of God in the Old Testament, they were used by Jesus and the writers of the New Testament both as prayers and also to demonstrate how the kingdom of God had been foretold. They have provided a language of worship for the Church ever since.

When we begin to use them in our prayers, we shall find that they encourage us to be ourselves before God. The thoughts and feelings of the psalmist echo our own, even across the boundaries of language, culture and time. Like us, he doubted the Lord's presence ('My God, my God, why have you forsaken me?'), felt he had been unfairly treated ('How long must I suffer anguish in my soul?'), thought the Lord had forgotten him ('Why do you hide your face from me in time of need?'), pleaded for help ('Hear the voice of my supplication when I cry to you'), complained of the callousness of others ('They repay me evil for good'), and begged for healing ('My loins are filled with a burning pain').

Paul regarded the psalms as the means whereby Spirit-filled disciples encourage one another and give thanks to God: 'Be filled with the Spirit. Speak to one another with the words of psalms, hymns, and sacred songs; sing hymns and psalms to the Lord with praise in your hearts. In the name of the Lord Jesus Christ, always give thanks for everything to God the Father' (Eph. 5: 18–20 TEV).

We shall also discern in them prophecies which prepare us for what God reveals to us through the Gospel, the Church, spiritual gifts, sacraments, and so on. References to the covenant, the temple, Mount Zion, the divine presence and the festivals can be related to the corresponding Christian realities: the new covenant, the eucharist, the presence of Christ in the incarnation, the Holy Spirit, and all that we celebrate in our faith.

John Chrysostom, Bishop of Constantinople (347–407) told his candidates for baptism that they should memorise the psalms so that they could praise God wherever they were and whatever they were doing at any time of the day.

4. The liturgy of the hours provides us with daily Bible readings. We are called to listen to the Word of God:

Oh, how I love thy law:
It is my meditation all the day (Ps. 119: 97).

We open the Bible at the selected passage. We read it slowly, alert for verses and phrases that attract our attention. We ponder its meaning, perhaps using our imagination to picture the scene if the passage is part of a narrative. We try to empty our minds of all thoughts except those which the printed words suggest.

Some days the passages mean little to us. We perhaps turn instead to another book, a devotional one, which we keep handy for such a moment. But on other days the passage comes alive as we reflect upon it. An idea, a prayer, a solution to a problem leaps into our minds. Of course, we test it. Does it conform to God's love and will? Is it devoid of evil and self-interest? Should we consult another Christian about it?

Through reading and reflecting on the scriptural passages, we open our minds and hearts to the Word of God. We expose ourselves to the renewing work of the Holy Spirit, who takes the things of God and reveals them to us. The inspiration of the written word in the Bible leads us to Jesus, the Word made flesh.

To have the mind of Christ is not to translate all that happens in and around us in biblical phraseology and thought-forms. Rather, it is to discern life with the eyes of the Spirit who thus leads us to see what glorifies the Lord and what denies him. What the scriptures do is enable us to see the works of God in the world as they were seen by the men and women of faith in the past. Their witness shows us how we can witness to the Gospel of the kingdom. Hence they become our daily bread.

When Paul gave his farewell address to the elders at Ephesus, he finished with these words: 'I commend you to the care of God and to the message of his grace, which is able to build you up and give you the blessings God has for all his people' (Acts 20: 32 TEV).

The care of God is his love and strength poured out to us in Jesus Christ. The message of his grace comes to us in his Word, spoken to us primarily through the scriptures which, by the Holy Spirit, have the power to build us up, to live as Christ's disciples, and to look for the coming of his kingdom.

The lectionary provided with Morning and Evening Prayer ensures that we read the whole Bible, not just the passages that appeal to us. One of the signs of the growing unity among Christians in this country is that many of them use this lectionary.

When I was in Romford, I belonged to a clergy fraternal which included Methodist, United Reformed and Baptist ministers as well as other Anglicans. In our prayers for the meeting we used the set passages. We sometimes compared notes for next Sunday's sermon! And when I prayed alone, I knew my friends were reflecting on the same biblical passages that day, too.

It is often worthwhile having a notebook handy to jot down any thoughts or prayers that come into your mind as a result of your reflection on the scriptures. They can be so useful for reference later.

5. At least once each day the liturgy of the hours directs us to an act of penitence, usually in the evening. We look back over the events of the day. Where have I been disobedient? Where have I failed to do what was required of me? Evangelical friends taught me the expression, 'Keeping short accounts with God'. Don't let sins go unconfessed. If you've offended somebody, apologise as soon as you can, and ask God's forgiveness that evening. We shall consider penitence in greater detail in a later chapter.

6. Finally, the liturgy of the hours encourages us to pray for one another and for all sorts and conditions of men. The intercessions usually come in the form of collects, litanies or periods of silence directed by the one who presides.

On the night of his betrayal Jesus prayed for his disciples and those who would come to believe in him through their apostleship – and that includes us. We, in union with him, intercede for one another and for all in any kind of need. 'The prayer of a righteous man has great power in its effects' (James 5: 16).

It's not easy to be organised in intercessions. For some years I kept a stiff-bound book with pages allocated for different days of the week; I noted down topics and requests for prayer on particular pages and kept the book with my Bible. Later I acquired a loose-leaf folder with coloured dividers; in it I put the various lists I received from missionary societies and other groups, and letters from friends. Recently I've relied on my memory. Perhaps it's time I used a book or a file again.

Various audio and visual aids are available, like the leaflets that have printed on them a scene, some verses of scripture, and a meditation. A diocesan bishop asked his clergy to send him a small photo of themselves. He put the photos in a book at his prayer-desk and looked at a number every day as he prayed for them. An old lady, who had wanted to be a missionary in China in her youth but had had to stay in England to look after ageing parents instead, made it her special ministry to pray for the Church there. She had a map of China printed on fabric. It had been made as a large table-cloth, but she spread it on the floor of her living-room and stood on one part of the map each day, praying that the Chinese in that part of their country would be won for Christ.

Students of Christian worship believe that the liturgy of the hours emerged in the second and third centuries A.D. out of the daily prayers of ordinary folks. What I've suggested here is a recovery of that daily devotion with the aid of the traditional framework which has been handed down to us.

I'm not suggesting that we should all use Morning and Evening Prayer. Many Christians do, in fact, use the liturgy of the hours and find the services a powerful aid to their discipleship. What I urge readers to do is to look at the revised rites as they have been published in recent years in the Anglican and Roman Catholic Churches (e.g., in the *Alternative Service Book*), learn why the (chiefly biblical) material has been assembled in such a manner, and then use what they feel might be helpful.

Daily devotions, whatever form they take, are intended to consecrate the whole of a Christian's life. In the rhythm of our encounters and activities, there are many opportunities for brief arrow prayers, moments of recollection, and offerings of spontaneous praise and thanksgiving to God. The morning and evening prayers of the individual act like the clasps at the ends of a chain of beads – they hold the chain together.

And as the months and years go by, we shall find that the distinction between praying and other things that we do each day becomes blurred. One activity will slip into another without losing our awareness of Christ's presence, and the day will become like a long-running act of praise.

The old name for the liturgy of the hours was the *opus dei*, 'the work of God'. It is a title that has often been coined to describe the act of praying.

But, when you come to think of it, the title will apply equally well to the business of daily Christian discipleship.

CHAPTER 4

The Hearts of the Fathers

The Old Testament begins with the story of how the first family which God created was torn asunder by sin when Cain murdered his brother; it ends with the prophecy that God will again restore the unity of the family: 'And he [the Lord] will turn the hearts of fathers to their children and the hearts of children to their fathers' (Mal. 4: 6).

Concern about the family has increased in the modern Church as the number of marriage breakdowns has risen in our society. The programme of congregations is filled with family services, family communions, family meetings and family suppers. There is greater care in preparing engaged couples for married life. The Church as the family of God is a dominant theme in contemporary teaching.

The restoration of loving relationships within the family is a fruit of the Holy Spirit. Indeed, the gift of the Spirit for that restoration is primary. Charisms such as speaking in tongues or words of knowledge shrink in significance when compared to the primary spiritual gift – the one which equips us to love and serve those we live with.

Ultimately the Church's teaching about the permanency of marriage does not depend on the vows taken by the bridegroom and the bride, important though they may be; it depends on our faith that God's grace never fails us if we are always open to him. Whatever else may be said about the causes of marriage breakdowns, in the end it is a sign that there has been a lack of forgiveness and an abandonment of grace within the relationship. God's love is not withdrawn. It is the response of the husband and the wife to that love which dies away and results in what is called 'the death of a marriage'.

The marriage relationship as a sphere within which the gifts of the Spirit operate lies behind the New Testament teaching on the family. One theme is that of the union of husband and wife as reflecting the union of Christ and his Church. The most famous exposition of this is in Ephesians 5: 32, where the redemption which Jesus brings is seen in terms of a bridegroom coming to claim his bride. The marriage service echoes this theme in its readings, hymns and prayers.

Another theme is that of the Christian family as a 'little church'. This theme has not been expounded as fully as the previous one in contemporary Christian teaching on the family, but it is particularly relevant today when we are rediscovering the spiritual strengths of small groups and house churches.

Paul regarded households as little churches. He greeted them as such: 'Greet Prisca and Aquila . . . also the church in their house' (Rom. 16. 3–5). It could be, of course, that he was not greeting just the people who lived together but also those who assembled in the house for worship and fellowship. Nevertheless, the principle remains. Where two or three are gathered together to form a Christian family, there is Jesus in the midst of them: and if we define the Church as an assembly of people who seek to follow Christ in commitment to one another, then even the nuclear family qualifies as a little church.

Pope John Paul II expressed this during one of his addresses in England in 1982:

The love of husband and wife in God's plan leads beyond itself and new life is generated, a family is born. The family is a community of love and life, a home in which children are guided to maturity. Marriage is a holy sacrament. Those baptised in the name of the Lord Jesus are married in his name also. Their love is a sharing in the love of God. He is its source. The marriages of Christian couples are images on earth of the wonder of God, the loving, life-giving communion of Three Persons in one God, and of God's covenant with Christ, with the Church.

Christian marriage is a sacrament of salvation. It is the pathway to holiness for all members of the family. With all my heart, therefore, I urge that your homes be centres of prayer; homes where families are at ease in the presence of God; homes to which others are invited to share hospitality, prayer and the praise of God: 'With gratitude in your hearts sing psalms and hymns and inspired songs to God; and never say or do anything except in the name of the Lord Jesus Christ, giving thanks to God the Father through him.'[1]

A Christian couple who came to put up their banns for marriage in the parish showed me an engagement ring with three gems on it.

'The middle one represents Jesus,' they told me. 'We want him to be between us in our life together.'

That is the primary spiritual gift – to equip the partners so that Christ is glorified between them. I was able to show them the prayer in the marriage service which asks the Lord to do this:

Lord and Saviour Jesus Christ,
who shared at Nazareth the life of an
    earthly home:
reign in the home of these your servants
    as Lord and King;
give them grace to minister to others
    as you have ministered to men,
and grant that by deed and word
they may be witnesses of your
    saving love
to those among whom they live;
for the sake of your holy name.

Outside marriage, one of the most committed forms of Christian congregation in the history of the Church has been the religious community. In Christian spirituality the religious life has been regarded as a parallel to married life – which is why some nuns are admitted to the religious community in a ceremony which is similar liturgically to a wedding service. One of the names for the religious community in medieval Latin was *familia*.

In the last chapter we drew from the traditions of the Church's worship to help us to learn how to pray. In this chapter I wish to draw from the traditions of the religious life to help us to learn how to live together. Like the liturgical traditions, those surrounding the religious life contain traces of the Spirit's wisdom which we can apply to ourselves today.

Since their emergence in the early centuries of Christian history, monks and nuns have had their lives framed on what are called the three evangelical counsels of poverty, chastity and obedience. These three virtues have been singled out as essential for those who want to follow the teaching ('counsel') of the Gospel ('evangelical').

Since they are the teaching of Jesus Christ, these evangelical counsels are, of course, binding on all Christians, but religious orders apply them to their community life in a systematic manner. They are the foundations of the various rules of the orders, like the Rule of St Benedict (sixth century), although they are applied in different ways – the Rule of St Francis (thirteenth century), for example, adopting an extremely simple life-style as an expression of evangelical poverty.

We shall look at each of these evangelical counsels in turn and discuss what we can learn from them to help us live by the Spirit in our homes.

Obedience

Controversy has raged long over the promise to obey in the

marriage service. Some Christians are unhappy that a woman should be regarded as completely equal to a man in the home, in the Church, and even in society. The opposition to their ordination in the Roman Catholic Church is matched in those Evangelical congregations where women are not allowed to be elders or to preside at services.

While Paul was influenced by the outlook of his time, when women were treated as inferior citizens, the implication of his teaching and that of the New Testament is that men and women are equal before God, complementing each other in their different roles – roles which may subtly change from one culture and age to another.

Nevertheless, their basic functions cannot change: fatherhood and motherhood belong to different sexes and call forth different gifts and responsibilities. The relationship of a husband and a wife has to contain both this equality and this complementarity. This was behind Paul's introductory injunction, 'Be subject to one another out of reverence for Christ' (Eph. 5: 21); other obediences mentioned by the apostle have to be understood against this general principle of mutual submission.

In a religious community this submission is given by the members to the superior, who is chosen by them as the one equipped by the Spirit to fulfil the role of pastoral leader to them. The Rule of St Benedict says, 'The abbot is believed to act in the place of Christ,' and remarks that the title 'abbot' is derived from *abba*, 'father'.[2] The community is not a democracy but an ordered company under a paternal leader. The same is true in convents where an abbess is the spiritual mother.

Transferred to a family, this pastoral leadership is shared in a complementary manner by the husband and wife together. When young men and women marry and become parents, their personalities frequently mature as they assume responsibilities for their home. It is the Christian belief that such maturing is crowned by gifts of the Holy Spirit to enable them to act in Christ's name as leaders of the family. In their different roles they fulfil a priestly ministry in pointing the members of the family to the real head of the household, Jesus Christ. I have already described how this affected me in my early years.

Such leadership has to be of a loving and persuasive kind, and the dictates of individual consciences have to be respected. Parental leadership promotes peace and order in the home. Visit any family where one parent dominates the other, or where there is no discipline in controlling the children, and see the difference!

Where two or more families join in forms of communal living, the differences between parental leadership can cause chaos. It is extremely difficult to control your own child if the parents of the other family don't control theirs, or if their standards and values are markedly different. Families sharing accommodation on holiday frequently experience this tension and are glad to return to their own homes! Modern, mixed communities experience the same problems.

If a Christian home cannot be run like a democracy, parental leadership must ensure that consultation takes place before important decisions are made. Openness to one another is vital if authority is to be respected. The commonest cause of marriage breakdowns is the drying up of consultation between husband and wife. 'We just couldn't talk to one another any more' is often heard in marriage guidance rooms and solicitors' offices.

The Rule of St Benedict directs:

> Whenever matters of importance have to be dealt with in the monastery, let the abbot summon the whole congregation and himself put forward the question that has arisen. Then, after hearing the advice of the brethren, let him think it over by himself and do what he shall judge most advantageous. Now we have said that all should be summoned to take counsel for this reason, that it is often to the younger that the Lord reveals what is best.[3]

A family I know with three children discuss together what they are going to do each day when they are away on holiday. One member makes his or her choice for one day in the week, and the rest accept it. If the mother wants to walk in the country, the others go with her; if the youngest wants to mess around on the beach, that is what they all do. The principle of consultation is extended to other matters concerning the family's life as well, although the final decision is made by the parents.

Today's permissive attitude is destructive for any community. It ignores the responsibility we have for one another. 'Each of us must consider his neighbour and think what is for his good and will build up the common life' (Rom. 15: 2 NEB). Husband and wife have the responsibility of affirming where boundaries are to be drawn in what is and what is not allowed in the home, and then they must support one another in upholding those rules.

But this will mean they must practise a disciplined life themselves. The mutual love and respect such a life generates has its effect on the rest of the family. This is essential, because although every effort is made to consult before decisions are taken, in practice parents have to make many decisions without consultation at all.

When the Barnabas Fellowship was founded in 1971 and a dozen of us began living together as a community at Whatcombe House, we assumed that we could do without rules. We would 'let the Spirit guide us'. But it didn't work. Certainly we sensed the Spirit's guidance in praying through certain issues of importance to the community; but in the 101 practical things of everyday life we had to adopt simple rules and allow the warden to exercise a personal leadership in making decisions for the rest of us.

In his exhortations to a Christian community, Paul wrote, 'admonish the idle, encourage the fainthearted, help the weak, be patient with them all' (I Thess. 5: 14). When should we speak of another's fault, and when should we be silent?

It's always good to have a frank talk with one another,

choosing the occasion carefully, rather than letting grievances pile up. But such talks must be in an atmosphere of
love. In dealing with rebelliousness, our own attitudes are
crucial. To put your arm across the shoulder of a teenage
daughter while explaining why she shouldn't go to an all-
night party is very different from facing one another in bitter
defiance.

And even if we're disobeyed, that's no reason for
abandoning our patience. We can wait for God to move in
the heart of the rebel while asking the Holy Spirit to remove
our hurt pride. After all, we disobey God often enough
ourselves! The Spirit can change people without our
intervention if we have patience.

So obedience in a loving community is not a crushing or
dehumanising thing. It is a liberation. Although mistakes
can be made by those who exercise parental leadership, we
can trust God to cope with the results of our misjudgments.
It doesn't do any of us harm to obey in something which
doesn't flout the will of God but with which we personally
disagree. In fact, it's a very practical way of learning to die a
little more to ourselves.

Chastity

The second of the evangelical counsels, chastity, means the
preservation of sexual purity according to our state of life –
virginity for the unmarried, loyalty to one's partner for the
married.

Chastity protects the dignity and worth of each
individual; it recognises that we are created for God's
purposes, not for our own.

'The body is not meant for immorality, but for the Lord,
and the Lord for the body. And God raised the Lord and will
also raise us up by his power. Do you not know that your
bodies are members of Christ?' (I Cor. 6: 13–15).

Popular attitudes in contemporary western society have

drifted far from this vision of human relationships. In drama, novels, plays and other forms of entertainment, it is widely assumed that sexual licence, homosexual as well as heterosexual, is right and proper if people are to be themselves. The practice of cohabitation is widespread (and even encouraged by the way income tax is assessed).

In recent decades the Church has succeeded in re-affirming the goodness of sex within the purposes of God, but it has not yet been so successful in reaffirming the fulfilment and freedom that chastity brings. This is partly because we are still confused by contemporary psycho-logical speculation and non-directive counselling, and partly because Church leaders who appear to condone permissiveness are more likely to be noticed by the media than those who uphold traditional Christian morals. The teaching of Pope Paul II on chastity, during his inter-national tours, has been a welcome corrective.

But in the end it is what Christians are in their personal lives which matters rather than what Christians leaders say (or don't say). The Christian family or community which upholds all that is enshrined in the evangelical counsel of chastity doesn't have to preach about it. In the neighbour-hood, in the workplace, in the parent-teacher association, in the evening class, in the hospital, in the political party, in the municipal council chamber – Christians who try to live chastely bring into their relationships a purity which speaks louder than words. By the power of the Spirit, our wayward desires can be cleansed and transformed until our lives begin to reflect the purity of Jesus Christ.

As in so much else, it is the lead given by the husband and the wife which creates the attitude in the home. Children soon recognise the weaknesses as well as the strengths of their parents. Reactions to dirty jokes, the use of language, the father's attitude towards other women and the mother's attitude towards other men – all those things affirm or deny chastity.

What this virtue means is that we offer ourselves, bodies

as well as minds and spirits, to God to be enjoyed by him. For this reason the total orientation of our sexuality towards the Holy Spirit is necessary along with everything else for our sanctification. In this way chastity gives us the freedom to surrender ourselves to God.

The promise of the bridegroom in the wedding service enshrines this evangelical counsel:

> With my body I honour you,
> all that I am I give to you,
> and all that I have I share with you,
> within the love of God,
> Father, Son and Holy Spirit.

There are two other things that should be said briefly about chastity.

The first is that the virtue includes respect and honour for another person as a human being created by God. Hence it rejects of all forms of violence against another, including attempts to manipulate them for our own purposes. There are strong sexual undercurrents in the urge to damage the mind and body of another – from cruel forms of interrogation to the ill-treatment of children. Muggings and throwing bottles at a football match are often at root symptoms of sexual frustration. 'Beastly' is an appropriate description of such behaviour: it is the result of unchecked animal-like instincts.

The second thing is that no matter how far we fall into sin in this area, as in any other, the forgiveness of Jesus Christ reaches out to us when we turn to him in penitence. Christ's treatment of the woman taken in adultery is a model for all time. To be forgiven is to be brought back into the place of renewal in the Spirit. There may be painful consequences we shall have to live with, but the Lord is able marvellously to use the experience of our human weakness in ministry to others if we grasp his forgiveness and submit to him more faithfully in the future.

Poverty

Nowadays we speak of Christian life-style rather than of poverty, but it is the same evangelical counsel we refer to. The glaring inequalities of wealth, power and privilege which we find in our society, and especially in the world, compel us to re-assess our attitudes to money and possessions in the light of the Gospel. 'For you know the grace of our Lord Jesus Christ, that though he was rich, yet for your sake he became poor, so that by his poverty you might become rich' (2 Cor. 8: 9). Paul saw the sharing of wealth, not just a matter of relieving the poor or of exercising a proper stewardship of our possessions, but of following the example of the Master – impoverishing ourselves for others, and being enriched by the sacrifice because through it we are brought close to Christ.

The religious community which demonstrated this virtue most strikingly was the Society of St Francis, founded in 1209 by the son of a rich cloth merchant in Assisi, who renounced his father's wealth in order to devote himself to prayer and the welfare of the poor. Although the Order of St Francis, in its Anglican as well as its Roman Catholic communities, engages in a wide variety of activities, the spirit of 'Lady Poverty' still pervades its life-style.

Yet the Rule of St Francis is careful not to make the pursuit of poverty an end in itself. It lays down that, when anyone wishes to join the brotherhood, 'the provincial minister shall tell them, in the words of the holy Gospel, to go and sell all that they have and carefully give it to the poor. But if they shall not be able to do this, their good will is enough. And the brothers shall be careful not to concern themselves about their temporal goods; so that they may freely do without these goods exactly as God inspires them.'[4]

In other words, it is the total surrender of what we have to God for his purposes which constitutes the spirit of poverty, not the giving away of everything.

Applied to the homes of Christian families, the Rule

underlines the New Testament attitude to material possessions and personal influence. The things we have and the power we possess belong to God, not to us. Tithing can become a mere law if we are content with just giving away one-tenth of what we earn. God is interested in what we do with the nine-tenths that we don't give away as well! The Old Testament standard can only be a rough-and-ready guide. There may be periods in our life when it is right to give away less; equally there may be other periods when it is right to give away much more.

The spirit of poverty involves putting to good use all that is available and not laying up unnecessary capital for fear of the future. It does not entail looking poverty-stricken. 'The spirit of poverty,' says the Rule of Taizé, 'means living in the joyfulness of each present day. If for God there is the generosity of distributing all the good things of the earth, for man there is the grace of giving what he has received.'

If we are buying a house, let us go for one that is livable in, not for one that is better than somebody else's. Purchase things for their usefulness rather than their status value. Do we really need to change that car for a more up-to-date model? Beware of special offers in shops that tempt you to buy the latest gadget you don't really require.

Most of us have far too many things. We accumulate clothes unnecessarily. Buy what you need, choose things of good quality, and wear them out. Hang the fashions! It's fashionable to ignore them, anyway! Practise the habit of giving things away. Once you're hooked on to that habit, you'll discover it really is more blessed to give than to receive!

When we moved house some years ago, I had to part with about half my books. There wasn't room for them without filling the rooms with shelves. It was a painful decision to make, because I can always persuade myself that I might need a book again one day! But once the cartons were delivered to the carrier's depot, I walked away feeling as if a burden had been taken from me. I had come out of the little prison I had made for myself and was enjoying the freedom.

Watch out for addictions – alcohol, aspirins, drugs, coffee, chocolate, tobacco. Don't be afraid to have a no-smoking ban in your home. If visitors are trying to kick the habit, they'll be grateful to you.

Try and take a special interest in some aspect of poverty in the world today. If you support Christian Aid or Tear Fund, pick out some area of the globe and look for opportunities to learn more about it. You may have a friend who is working in an African, Latin American or Asian country, where there is deprivation of different kinds. Discover its extent and what causes it. Then you will not just be contributing to yet another appeal for the hungry; you will be giving deliberately knowing something of what it is for. The same applies to aspects of poverty in our own country. If we are to pray as well as to give – the two are linked together in Christian spirituality – we need to be informed. Organisations like those just mentioned supply visual aids and other materials to assist families and groups to do this.

Besides the three evangelical counsels, the religious life is also governed with the division of the day into prayer, work, recreation and rest. The programme of communities' houses is drawn up with this in mind.

The tradition has much to teach any Christians, whether they live in families, in communities or alone. It is well worth while sitting down and reviewing how far our lives are distributed between those four headings.

If we have managed to create a space in our lives for daily prayer, we shall want to allocate a portion of that time for praying together. The expression 'family prayers' conjures up in my mind a more leisurely age with the domestic staff assembled with the family, while the head of the house reads from the Bible – an upstairs-downstairs picture. Nowadays households seem to be less orderly establishments with individuals coming and going at different times.

However difficult it might be to engage children in corporate prayer when they grow up (and the best many can do in the teenage phase is to say grace before the evening meal), it is important that the husband and wife maintain the discipline themselves. Even if it is only on one evening a week that they sit down together, discuss their affairs, and pray about them, that will help to preserve a citadel of God's peace in the midst of a busy household.

We can look for opportunities for spontaneous prayer. Conversation can be steered into prayer when appropriate. In a discussion, suggest you offer the matter to God there and then. Or if you've been enjoying something together, like an expedition into the country, say a prayer of thanksgiving to God when everyone is back in the car before you switch on the engine. Popular choruses also provide us with a means of praising God in all sorts of circumstances.

Work includes all that a family does round the house, individually and together. Children need to be encouraged to take their share of the domestic jobs; teaching them how to handle tools and equipment properly is more rewarding than fobbing them off with expensive toys.

Recreation includes the time we spend in enjoying ourselves. Discover what the family can do together at different ages – walking, cycling, swimming, tennis. Make a point of checking how long you spend with the children each day. Do you always say you're too busy when they ask you to help with the Lego?

And don't surrender every day to the TV. Look out for ways in which the family can create its own entertainment.

Worship is not only a matter of family prayers and Sunday services. A Jewish rabbi told me that his faith in God had taken root, not in the gatherings in the synagogue, but in the joyful occasions in his home when the sabbath or a festival was celebrated.

On Friday evening when he was a boy the family would sit round the table in their best clothes. His mother would light the candles and recite a Hebrew blessing. His father would pronounce the blessings over the wine and over the *challot*, the twisted loaves of white bread. Songs would be sung. The following day the family would relax together (his parents were not strict Orthodox Jews and their interpretation of what should or what should not be allowed on the sabbath was liberal).

Trapped by the television, we are in danger of losing the gift of celebration from our homes. In our culture we think of going out for a meal, visiting the theatre or the pub. Entertainment has become utterly secularised.

The Christian family needs Christian family celebrations. Weekends can be used to do things together in which all participate. The festivals of the Church's year can be marked at home by Christian pictures and symbols, special treats on the table for which God is thanked in the grace. Candles, Bible readings, songs – let the birthday, the wedding anniversary, the end of decorating the dining-room, be occasions of rejoicing in which God's presence and goodness is honoured.

Organise your own acts of worship, especially on Sundays when it isn't possible to go to church. Set bread and wine on the table and let father and mother together preside over a simple domestic eucharist, using some of the prayers from the service book.

Don't imagine your children's concept of God will be the same as your own. We have much to learn from children's religious experience. They often have a happy, attentive and wholehearted appreciation of the heavenly Father, with a wonder and a joy at the presence of Jesus Christ, which we miss if we don't spend time listening to and sharing with them.

Grown-ups forget what it is like to be a child. Not long ago I went back to the school I attended when I was ten or eleven. I had not visited it since I left it just before the war. I was amazed how small it was. In my memory it had been a huge, rambling place with vast playing-fields. That's how different a child's approach to religion and life is: a different scale of values, a different angle on things.

They can praise God uncomplicated by our dogmas, fears and doubts.

'Hurry up and say a little prayer to Jesus. Mummy's got lots to do before she goes to bed tonight!'

What could be more discouraging than a remark like that? A little prayer supposes a little faith and a little God. But a child's longing and imagination is for a big, all-powerful God, radiant with light. Prayers should begin with praises and thanksgivings; confessions of sin and intercessions should be sincere but brief. And trust the Holy Spirit to lead your children in prayer. You'll only have to follow their lead – and you'll learn a lot!

Answer questions about God simply, using words and examples that are familiar to them. If you don't know the answer, say so; children are rarely disappointed if an adult doesn't know something – it gives them a sense of solidarity with the parent if the latter is as puzzled as they are.

Rely on the Spirit to guide you in your dealings with them. Ask for love, joy and peace in everything that concerns them, especially their spiritual awakening. Don't be overawed by the psychological theories that you pick up from papers, magazines and broadcasts. Live happily with your children, love them, be joyful with them, and don't succumb to anxieties or feel guilty about mistakes! If things go wrong one day, start the next day with a clean slate.

If you discover that looking after them exposes weaknesses in yourself – bursts of anger, waves of self-pity – go into their bedroom when they are asleep and pray by their beds that God will give you the grace of the opposite virtue to enable you to turn your back on those weaknesses. And then thank him for the children before you leave the room.

Disagreements and rows happen from time to time in the best families. If one happens between you and your husband/wife/relative/friend/child in the presence of the children, make sure they are present when you say sorry to one another. That will teach them more about love than almost anything else they experience in the home.

[1] *The Pope Teaches* (Catholic Truth Society, 1982), p. 188.
[2] David Parry, *Households of God* (Darton, Longman and Todd, 1980), p. 17.
[3] Ibid, pp. 161-2.
[4] Henry Bettenson, *Documents of the Christian Church* (Oxford, 1946), p. 179.

CHAPTER 5

A Dwelling Place for God

I shall always remember my first night in Romford. The year was 1958. I had been appointed parish priest in Rush Green, and I had moved into the little terrace house which in those days served as the vicarage. Friends from the parish where I had been a curate had brought me over and helped me to unpack and to prepare a meal. Eventually they had said their goodbyes and departed.

It was then I realised, with a sense of cold shock, that I was to live alone for the first time in my life.

When I went to bed in the empty house, I pulled back the curtains and looked out at the lighted windows of my neighbours' homes. I did not know it then, but I was to live there by myself for the next thirteen years.

According to statistical surveys, more than a quarter of the people in Britain over the age of 40 live by themselves in houses or flats. Look down the road where you live and you will soon see what this means. In the six houses close to where I am typing this book, three are the homes of women who live alone.

So there are lots of lonely people about.

Some are widowers and widows. Theirs is a sad experience of solitariness. Although a happy marriage leaves its memories and sense of thankfulness, life is never the same again – unless a second marriage offers a new beginning, a new sense of being wanted and loved. Others are alone because they have been separated or divorced. For them the loneliness of the house can seem like a penalty for a personal failure, no matter how relieved they are that tensions in relationships have been removed.

And others are men and women who, for a variety of reasons, have never married. As the years slip by, they slowly come to realise that marriage is not to be theirs. For women especially, the sight of other women with husbands and children can be a prickling reminder of their loneliness. Such men and women may feel in different ways that something precious in life has passed them by.

Few of us choose a solitary existence. But when we find ourselves in this situation, we tend to become absorbed in our jobs, in our family and friends, in tasks around the congregation, and in leisure activities or good causes of one kind or another.

But there is always the emptiness of our house to face when we come home. Sometimes that can be a relief! But at other times it is cold and unwelcoming, especially when we've spent the evening in the company of others. We are aware of the burden of looking after the building. There's no one to share in the responsibility for making decisions about repairs, alterations, decorations. We feel vulnerable, particularly when we're ill. We're liable to become very dependent on the radio, the TV, the telephone.

What does it mean to live by the Spirit in these circumstances?

In this process of accepting our circumstances the rhythm of prayer is essential. Alone we have the advantage of being able to plan how we spend our time at home without distractions from others – provided there are not too many callers!

People who live by themselves can be aware of God's presence in the house in a deeply personal way. Hours of silence provide opportunities for talking to the Lord and listening to him which are less available when we live with others. We know God as a constant companion in every activity as our home becomes a dwelling place for him.

Gradually we experience the healing grace of God. That is

one of the fruits of a discipline of prayer. Bitter thoughts, despairing hopes, personal anxieties, do not have to be crushed. We can bring them each day to God, speaking them aloud, if we want to. Wisps of the bitterness, the despair and the anxiety will drift over our consciousness now and then, but they will no longer master us. In us a power is mastering them, and they are replaced by a growing awareness of God's love. With the psalmist we want to cry, 'Whom have I in heaven but thee? And there is nothing upon earth that I desire besides thee' (Ps. 73: 25).

This can be true, too, of those who find themselves alone after the death of a husband or wife, a child or a parent. The parting leaves a scar that remains for the rest of our lives. But scars can be signs of healing as well as indications of past hurts.

Christians who live alone share with Jesus Christ in his withdrawal from the world, when he communed with his heavenly Father and sought guidance and strength for the next stage of his ministry. In this withdrawal he followed the example of Moses, who met God in the desert in the burning bush and on Mount Sinai, and Elijah, who encountered God on the mountain. Throughout the history of the Church, God has called certain men and women to share in that experience of being alone with him. Antony of Egypt and Julian of Norwich were two such disciples – Antony in the desert, Julian in her anchorite's cell in Norwich. Those who live alone can learn from their ministries of prayer, teaching and service to others.

Today the Russian word, *poustinia* (pronounced poo-steem-yah), is used of this discipline of withdrawal: the place away from the mainstream of modern life, the lonely spot where we are better able to hear God's Word and reflect upon it. We all need our *poustinia*, whether we live alone or with others. It may be a room or a corner – a secret place of escape, like the bathroom that the girl went into for her prayers. For the Christian who lives alone, the *poustinia* is always available.

The liturgy of the hours can become a powerful support to us. We keep our Bible and prayer-book in a favourite spot and sit there for our appointment with the Lord each morning and evening. When we no longer go out to work, we can arrange our day round these services, supplementing them, for instance, with broadcasts of Evensong from cathedrals on the BBC.

Some parish churches maintain the custom of saying the liturgy of the hours on weekdays – or at least saying one of the services each day. In areas where there are retired people, it is not unusual to find a small congregation in church each day. I know several parishes where the liturgy of the hours is maintained in church by Christians who have the time to offer this ministry, especially those who live alone.

Those of us who live or have lived by ourselves while following an active career react against the assumption many married people have that we have more leisure time than they. Out at work all day, we come home, prepare a meal, cope with the housework, the garden, the laundry, the decorating, and go to bed exhausted. Having experienced both kinds of existence, I can testify that one is not more leisurely than the other!

But single people have greater freedom to undertake ministries away from home which are not possible for those with young families. And when they retire, they are in a position to offer help in the many jobs that surround an average congregation.

It is particularly important that those who live alone should belong to at least one Christian group in which they feel at home. It becomes their spiritual family. The group enables them to share concerns and to receive help in times of crisis. The pastoral leadership in any congregation has a special responsibility to encourage the formation of such groups as a ministry to the single people in its membership. The nature of the group may vary according to circumstances in the congregation: it may be a prayer or Bible study group, or it may be a more informal gathering.

Some single people find themselves drawn into the fellowship of one or two families. During my years in Romford, I was grateful for various married friends who invited me into their homes and who never seemed put out when I rang up and asked if I could spend an evening with them. Those who are single, however, have to be sensitive to the needs of the family concerned: there will be times when a visitor is not so welcome.

Those who are alone can form their own groups, too. Four or five meet together on a regular basis for meals in one another's homes. This is an economic and pleasant way of sharing the cost of a dinner at weekends or during retirement. I have met such groups who spend a whole day each week together, taking it in turn to prepare the meals or going on joint outings.

Visitors enable you to practise Christian hospitality. Friends used my vicarage as a bed-and-breakfast lodging when coming to London; occasionally I provided a bed for those who were coming to the diocese or to the local council of churches from overseas on furlough. The near-by Samaritan branch asked me to give a bed to clients now and then: usually this was a privilege, although I eventually had to refuse disturbed families, who tended to take over my house with their children and pet animals and regard it as their own property! It was also necessary to bar certain unaccompanied members of the opposite sex!

Friends' children stayed during the holidays. It is good to have kids around the house. They give us a different perspective on the way we live – and on our attitude towards pieces of precious furniture!

My mother, who has lived alone for several years, offers her home to the parish for meetings. Hardly a week goes by without her sitting-room being crowded with a prayer-meeting or a sub-committee.

Visitors can be invited to join in your routine of prayer, when it is appropriate for them to do so.

The life of Jesus presents single Christians with a model that is very relevant to them. In his time it was extremely unusual for a man in his position to be unmarried. Yet by remaining celibate, he was able to give himself in ministry to others in a depth that would hardly have been possible if he had been married.

And although he was single, he was able to relate to women and children with great freedom and intimacy because his motives were utterly unselfish and centred on obedience to God. There was never a hint of scandal about those relationships. He only said and did what the Father wanted him to say and do.

His celibacy was a spiritual gift. The anointing of the Holy Spirit at the river Jordan equipped him in this as well as in other powers to proclaim the Gospel of the kingdom of God. There was no question of a lack of fulfilment in his life. Today, in our permissive society, we too easily assume that sexual intimacy with another is a necessary condition of our psychological and physical fulfilment. The example of Jesus refutes that. Our fulfilment is the same as his: in obedience to the Father – an obedience in union with Christ by the power of the same Spirit who anointed him. That is the mark of belonging to his family: 'Whoever does the will of God is my brother, and sister, and mother' (Mark 3: 35).

Today we have lost the understanding of celibacy as a calling by God. The spiritual gift – for that is what it is when it is accepted 'for the sake of the kingdom of heaven' (Matt. 19: 12) – has become a missile in the debate about allowing Roman Catholic priests to marry. Yet Christians who are single or who live alone should seek the guidance of the Holy Spirit to see if this may be their calling, especially when it seems unlikely that they will marry. It could be a key to contented acceptance of their situation.

There is a memorable piece of writing in Michel Quoist's *Prayers of Life*, which reveals the struggle towards that contented acceptance in the heart of a man who has to be celibate because of his office in the Roman Catholic Church.

It is a lesson for all of us, married or single.

The prayer is in the form of a dialogue between the priest and God. The priest has returned to his presbytery at the end of a busy Sunday. It is an evening in the week when his loneliness is more obvious to him because he has been with people all day. In the silence of his room his thoughts turn to the folk he has met – especially those delightful youngsters whom, he sadly reflects, can never be his own.

Like the psalmist, he turns his sadness into prayer:

I've given you all, but it's hard, Lord.
It's hard to give one's body; it would like to give itself
    to others.
It's hard to love everyone and to claim no one.
It's hard to shake a hand and not want to retain it.
It's hard to inspire affection, to give it to you.
It's hard to be nothing to oneself in order to be
    everything to others.

Then he hears the Lord gently replying:

> Son, you are not alone.
> I am with you.
> I am you.
> I needed another human vehicle to continue
>   my incarnation and redemption.
> Out of all eternity, I chose you.
> I need you.

Realising afresh the love of God, the priest surrenders himself once more to his calling:

Here I am, Lord,
Here is my body,
Here is my heart,
Here is my soul.
Grant that I may be big enough to reach the world...

I repeat to you my 'yes' – not in a burst of laughter,
  but slowly, clearly, humbly,
Alone, Lord, before you
In the peace of the evening.[1]

I once introduced a Roman Catholic priest who was a
Franciscan friar to the pastor of an Evangelical church.
They co-operated over a number of projects and became
friends, visiting one another, playing golf together. Eventually the friar was sent overseas by his superiors and the
pastor attended the farewell eucharist.

Some months later I met the pastor, and in the course of
our conversation he remarked that the Franciscan was one
of the most remarkable Christians he had ever met.

'What was it about him that struck you?' I asked.

He thought for a moment.

'What struck me,' he said, 'was that this man had no one in
his life but Jesus. No family, no possessions, no income –
just Jesus, with complete freedom to serve him.'

A different form of loneliness is experienced by Christians
who live with those who do not or cannot share their faith.
The commonest situation is where a husband or a wife is a
Christian and the partner is not.

The Churches try, in different ways, to encourage their
younger members to marry within the Christian fellowship.
The difficulties which are sometimes experienced in
arranging marriages between Roman Catholics and other
Christians should not obscure the fact that the Roman
Catholic Church takes positive and evangelistic steps to
ensure that if one of its members marries a non-Catholic, the
latter is given a chance to understand what his or her future
partner believes. How the opportunity is handled varies
from parish to parish, but many Roman Catholics I have
met were baptised and/or confirmed because of their
encounter with the Christian faith in their future partner and
in the priest who prepared them for marriage.

Nevertheless, in the local church and prayer-group we meet the man or the woman who is the only member of the Christian fellowship in their household.

What can we say to a wife in this position? (For a husband, the same suggestions apply.)

1. Avoid falling into the error of imagining that you possess God in some way the other doesn't. Remember, we don't possess God; he calls us and, if we respond, he possesses us. God is the Lord of all the earth, and he is the Lord of your husband, even if your husband doesn't realise this and acknowledge him. So don't put God on to your side of your married life and assume that he isn't working on your husband's side as well. Indeed, if your husband really loves you, I doubt whether you will be able to sustain that error for long!

2. Don't set up a barrier between your husband and yourself in your Christian outlook. It is true that one who believes in Jesus Christ as Lord and Saviour is in a different realm of grace from one who doesn't. 'There is therefore now no condemnation for those who are in Christ Jesus' (Rom. 8: 1). The sin of unbelief remains in your husband as long as he refuses to come to Christ.

But the difference between you and him in these matters isn't as simple as that. As I tried to illustrate in the first chapter, the reasons why we come to faith are usually very complex. The Spirit of God uses all kinds of agencies in our lives to bring us to the moment when we accept Jesus as Lord. Many Christians – and it is difficult to deny that they are Christians – hesitate on the margin of doubt and faith, influenced more by their upbringing and the kind of people they move among than by a considered personal decision. Eventually they grow into a more committed faith, but the pilgrimage never ends. There are times when all of us retreat to the margin of doubt again and have to be reorientated to the Holy Spirit once more.

3. Few men and women totally and finally reject belief in God and act consistently with their atheism. Many who

describe themselves as agnostics are in their hearts seeking the truth. Most have a sincere respect for the Christian faith. If the Christians they had met had been better witnesses to the risen Lord in their lives, those men and women would perhaps have been converted by now.

So learn to look for the signs of God's goodness in your husband's life. The Holy Spirit will be at work in him. Is he kind and generous towards you? Does he share in your married life fairly and unselfishly? Is he open-hearted towards others, willing to go the extra mile? Has he a concern for underprivileged people, in the neighbourhood or abroad? Is he active in local political life? There is so much in him to thank God for! Make that one of the reasons why you praise God when you are worshipping with other Christians. Hold your husband up before the Lord with thanksgiving. Let that prayer come first before any thoughts of interceding for his conversion!

4. Don't think that your first priority is to get him to come to church. There may be occasions when it is right to suggest he comes with you, if there is some special event – a well-known preacher or a series of songs led by the choir your children are in – but ration the number of times you make that suggestion. (On the other hand, don't neglect it. On several occasions such husbands have said to me, 'I didn't go to church in the past because my wife never invited me!')

Rather, let the subject of the Christian faith come up naturally in the course of your conversation together. If possible, let the initiative come from him. Items of news on the TV, the family's celebration of the Christian festivals, the worksheets that the children bring home from Sunday school – these can be taken up around the basic question, 'What does Jesus Christ mean in our lives?' Steer clear of head-on clashes of opinion. If you have to express disagreement, do so, explaining your reasons, but avoid an argument about it. Try as far as possible to support what he says – and indicate that you do so, not just as a dutiful wife, but as a disciple of Christ.

Attacks on the Church by your husband are sometimes difficult to handle. You will feel resentful that your loyalties to the congregation are being challenged. But make allowances for the fact that there is still much in the Church which obscures rather than proclaims the Gospel. We who are members so often get in Christ's way! Some Church leaders are unwise in what they say publicly. If your husband's criticism of the Church is just, agree with him, but then go on to point out that on the Christian pilgrimage we frequently fall by the wayside and have to rely on the love and power of God to set us on our way again.

5. Beware of disloyal affections for other men in the congregation who seem so much better Christians than your husband. In times of difficulty it is easy to fall into the error of feeling that you made a mistake in marrying him and that the Lord is giving you a chance to rectify it. There is greater freedom in relationships between the sexes in congregations as well as in society, and the intimacy of prayer-groups has its dangers as well as its strengths.

I met a middle-aged couple at a conference on shared ministries. I noticed they behaved affectionately towards one another and I felt glad for the blessings such conferences have for married people when they can get away together.

At coffee-time one morning they took up the subject of the complementary roles of men and women in counselling. I had been explaining in the lecture how in some situations a man and woman can act as a team.

They stood in front of me with their arms round one another's waists telling me how the Lord had used them in partnership in helping various people.

'Have you always done this since you were married?' I asked.

There was a slight hesitation and a change of expression on their faces.

'Oh, we're not married,' said the man. 'My wife's not a Christian, so she couldn't do these things with me.'

'Neither's my husband,' blurted out the woman.

They broke off the conversation and walked away. They seemed to keep away from me for the rest of the conference.

6. Remember, if Christ is acknowledged in a home only by one member of it, then the kingdom of God is beginning to break through into the lives of all in the house. And act in that faith. Assume that your husband will always support you in upholding what you know is right. Get him to share in some way in the religious upbringing of the children. Let him read Bible stories to them; let him share in the prayers. When questions arise about daddy not going to church, don't try to cover up; let him explain his reasons himself.

In 1 Corinthians where Paul discussed the marriage of Christians with unbelievers, the apostle wrote, 'The unbelieving husband is consecrated through his wife, and the unbelieving wife is consecrated through her husband. Otherwise, your children would be unclean, but as it is they are holy' (1 Cor. 7: 14). It is a passage commentators find difficult to explain. J. B. Phillips translated it, 'The unbelieving husband is, in a sense, consecrated by being joined to the person of his wife'; the *New English Bible*, 'The heathen husband now belongs to God through his Christian wife'; the *Today's English Version*, 'The unbelieving husband is made acceptable to God by being united to his wife.' None of them avoids giving the impression that one can become a Christian not only by being baptised but also by being married to a Christian! Unless Paul was toying with the notion that the baptismal covenant could be extended across the marriage bond irrespective of the beliefs of one of the partners (and that's highly unlikely), then the most natural interpretation is that when a Christian wife constantly submits herself to the Holy Spirit, then God comes among all those in her home in a loving and powerful way.

There are many other kinds of loneliness in our society

today. You can live with others and still be isolated as a Christian.

There is the woman who is trapped at home by the need to look after elderly and unbelieving relatives. It can be an exhausting existence, especially if they are bitter or mentally ill. The choice of whether to keep them at home or to hand them into care is not an easy one to make.

There is the student who is the only Christian in a hostel or college. I've met several young people over the years who've gone up to a university with eager anticipation and then by the end of their first year come home detesting the experience. I've discovered it wasn't their work that disheartened them, but the conduct of those who lived on the same staircase or corridor – drunkenness, drug-taking, immorality, and so on.

There is the mother of a single-parent family whose work and care of her children leave her little time for joining in congregational life.

And there is the loneliness of the parents whose energies are spent in caring for a disabled child. Often they are tempted to cut themselves off from others in the neighbourhood and in the congregation because they feel their handicapped offspring requires the whole of their attention and that somehow they are less acceptable socially because of him or her.

To live by the Spirit in such difficult situations of loneliness requires the same pattern of obedience to God that we have been examining: a surrender to God of the feelings of helplessness and bitterness; an inner acceptance of the situation believing that that is where God wants us at the moment; an invocation of the Holy Spirit for the gifts and graces we need to cope with the opportunities and demands that come our way each day; and a trust in Jesus Christ that from among his people he will send those who can support and encourage us.

I met a woman recently whose husband had deserted her

when the youngest of her five children had been two years old.

Yes, she admitted, it had been hard at first – extremely hard. But through the experience she had learned to depend on the Lord as she had never done before. Now her children were grown up and launched on careers, some of them married with children of their own.

'They're my five best friends,' she told me simply, 'and I couldn't ask for a greater gift from God than that.'

[1] Michel Quoist, *Prayers of Life* (Gill and Son, 1963), pp. 50–1.

CHAPTER 6

One With Another

We Christians make great claims for the Church. The New Testament images of the Church – the people of God, the body of Christ, the fellowship of the Holy Spirit, the vine, the new temple – are expounded in sermons and books to teach us that belonging is to be members of a company which has Jesus Christ as its head. To be joined to him in this way (to be 'in Christ', using the apostle Paul's favourite expression), we are told, is to be in a union with God which endures beyond death itself.

Yet when we look round at our own local congregation with its problems, its jealousies and its divisions, we might well wonder if it is the same thing that we are hearing about. Can this really be the same New Testament Church?

To answer that, go back to the New Testament itself. Nearly half of it is made up of letters written to congregations founded in the decades after Pentecost. These were the actual local churches that the apostles and others experienced as they were teaching about the people of God, the body of Christ, the fellowship of the Holy Spirit, the vine, the new temple.

When we study those letters we find that, again and again, the apostolic writers had to recall the congregations to repentance, to faithfulness, and to renewal, in the name of Jesus Christ.

'I appeal to you, brethren, to take note of those who create dissensions and difficulties' (Rom. 16: 17) – 'Keep your life free from love of money, and be content with what you have'

(Heb. 13: 5) – 'Do not speak evil against one another' (Jas. 4: 11) – 'Practise hospitality ungrudgingly to one another' (1 Pet. 4: 9) – 'Keep his commandments' (1 John 3: 24) – 'You have abandoned the love you had at first' (Rev. 2: 4).

In the book of Acts we are shown the Spirit-filled Church marching in the triumph of the Gospel from Jerusalem to Rome, manifesting gifts of worship, community-sharing, evangelism, prophecy, teaching, martyrdom and hospitality. Yet within its fellowship there was also greed and deceit (5: 1–11), jealousies (6: 1), an attempt to trade in spiritual gifts (8: 9–24), and a quarrel between two of its outstanding leaders, Paul and Barnabas (15: 36–41).

Corinth, the New Testament congregation of which we know a good deal through Paul's letters, was plagued with sins: disunity, spiritual pride, sexual immorality, neglect of the poor, members taking one another to court, disorder at the eucharist, false teachers, rejection of apostolic oversight. There can't be many present-day churches in a worse state than that (though my friends tell me that when a congregation begins moving with the Holy Spirit, the devil gets active, too, and the Corinthian scene becomes credible!)

Yet Paul could still say of the Corinthian Christians that they were 'called to be saints' (1 Cor. 1: 2), 'God's temple . . . God's Spirit dwells in you' (3: 16), 'Christ's' (3: 23), and 'the body of Christ' (12: 27).

He wasn't being tactful – or optimistic! He said these things because he practised what he preached. He urged the congregation to accept the fruit of the Spirit – faith, hope and love (13. 13) – and he looked at them with faith, hope and love himself. Because he was open to the Spirit, he saw them through the eyes of Jesus Christ.

The apostle's viewpoint, if we may call it that, is such an important model for us when we look at our own local congregation that we must examine it in more detail. Various texts in the Corinthian correspondence help us to see how he arrived at it.

From the scriptures Paul knew that in the past God had

been faithful to the covenant he had made through Moses with Israel, in spite of their many backslidings and disobediences. He knew that the story of Israel pointed forward prophetically to the new and greater covenant God made with his people through Jesus Christ. On this basis the apostle could look at the Corinthians with faith in what God had done for them. The scriptures had been fulfilled in Christ's death and resurrection. 'And he died for all, that those who live might live no longer for themselves but for him who for their sake died and was raised' (2 Cor. 5: 15).

Through baptism they had been incorporated into the Church and brought within the sphere of God's saving activity. 'For by one Spirit we were all baptised into one body – Jews or Greeks, slaves or free – and all were made to drink of one Spirit' (1 Cor. 12: 13). As the old Israel had been given water from the rock in the desert by God, so the new Israel had been given the Holy Spirit by him for its pilgrimage as Christ's disciples through this life.

The Corinthians celebrated this new covenant in eating the bread and in drinking the wine of the Lord's Supper (1 Cor. 11: 24–5). They were already en route for the destiny God had prepared for them. Since Christ had died for them according to the scriptures (15: 3), Paul could urge them to 'sin no more' (15: 34) because they were 'sanctified in Christ' (1: 2). What God had accomplished could now be effective in their lives through the power of the cross (1: 18). Therefore they should 'Be watchful, stand firm in your faith, be courageous, be strong' (16: 13).

Added to this faith was Paul's hope that God would fulfil his purposes in the Corinthian congregation, in spite of the signs of their disobedience. The new covenant had inaugurated a new age. 'Therefore, if anyone is in Christ, he is a new creation; the old has passed away, behold, the new has come' (2 Cor. 5: 17). The sin that remained among them could only be the last efforts of the evil one who was already defeated.

This meant that the apostle could look expectantly for indications of God's grace among the Corinthians. And he saw it. He seems to have had great respect for their leaders. He mentioned warmly the household of Stephanas, the first converts who had devoted themselves to the service of the Church, and he was encouraged when Stephanas visited him with Fortunatus and Achaicus (1 Cor. 16: 15–18).

He praised God for them all.

I give thanks to God always for you because of the grace of God which was given you in Christ Jesus, that in every way you were enriched in him with all speech and all knowledge – even as the testimony to Christ was confirmed among you – so that you are not lacking in any spiritual gift, as you wait for the revealing of our Lord Jesus Christ; who will sustain you to the end, guiltless in the day of our Lord Jesus Christ. God is faithful, by whom you were called into the fellowship of his Son, Jesus Christ our Lord (1 Cor. 1: 4–9).

Paul wrote to them sharply about their faults and ordered the excommunication of a grievous offender. Persistent, serious sin was not to be tolerated within the fellowship, if the guilty person would not repent. But his reproofs were uttered out of a thankfulness to God for what he had already accomplished and in the hope of further grace to come. So he could also encourage them to join him in imitating Christ and to rejoice that 'we . . . are being changed into his likeness from one degree of glory to another; for this comes from the Lord who is the Spirit' (2 Cor. 3: 18).

Notice the last ten words. They underline the truth that our efforts may be feeble, unsuccessful, even shameful; but if we are open to the Spirit of God, he will work the transformation in us by his power. That is why the apostle was not dismayed by what he heard from Corinth. 'I have great confidence in you; I have great pride in you; I am filled with comfort' (2 Cor. 7: 4).

His faith and hope in what God had done, was doing, and was going to do in that congregation was crowned with his love for them, '. . . our heart is wide' (2 Cor. 6: 11). In Acts 18 we read how Paul founded the Church in Corinth after eighteen difficult months, helped by his friends, Aquila and Priscilla. His letters glow with his affectionate concern for this mixed crowd of converted Jews and Greeks, mostly ordinary people who made up the congregation. He had a deep, paternal feeling for them; they were his 'workmanship in the Lord' (1 Cor. 9: 1).

But human affection would hardly have sustained him through all the disappointments they brought him. It was God's love that flowed through him towards them. 'I feel a divine jealousy for you, for I betrothed you to Christ to present you as a pure bride to her one husband' (2 Cor. 11: 2).

It may have been this sense of divine love that wrung from him the exquisite poem which occupies the famous chapter thirteen of the first letter. When he described love as bearing all things, believing all things, hoping all things, enduring all things, was he describing his own experience of loving the Corinthians in the anxieties they caused him? When he spoke of the thorn in the flesh which harassed him, was he linking what is thought to have been a physical ailment with the hurt caused by the Corinthians, so that he was able to surrender that congregation, with his illness, to the Lord?

He had been given a word from the Lord, perhaps through a gift of prophecy: 'My grace is sufficient for you, for my power is made perfect in weakness' (2 Cor. 12: 9). That word could have been about his relationships with them, too. So in love he could send them a holy kiss with his greetings: 'The grace of the Lord Jesus Christ and the love of God and the fellowship of the Holy Spirit be with you all' (2 Cor. 13: 14). As we have already noted, that text sums up the whole Gospel of God as he reaches out through the Son to save us by his Spirit. Paul saw the Corinthian Church within that perspective of God's coming kingdom.

How, then, does Paul's attitude towards this congregation compare with our attitude towards our local church?

Looking round them on Sundays, we see some whom we

recognise as outstanding Christians. Their humility, their simple life-style, their spiritual gifts – clearly they are numbered among the saints.

And we see those for whom we are particularly grateful to God: friends we love to be with, the preacher whose sermons helped us to come to faith in Jesus Christ, the couple who prayed with us through a personal crisis and through whom we felt the healing touch of the Spirit.

And then we see others we don't know very well... and one or two we don't like very much...

At this point we pause. All these people are our brothers and sisters in the Lord – whether we happen to like them or not. They are God's choice, not ours.

We are made one in Christ with them. It isn't a case of *them* and *us*. Salvation is corporate – like prayer. We come to Christ individually through repentance and faith, but baptism in water and in the Holy Spirit unites us with one another.

The unity we receive through initiation into the Church is expressed vividly in the service of baptism and confirmation in the Church of England, when the bishop says to the candidates, 'God has received you by baptism into his Church,' and the congregation join in:

> We welcome you into the Lord's family.
> We are members together of the body of Christ;
> we are children of the same heavenly Father;
> we are inheritors together of the kingdom of God.
> We welcome you.

One of the authentic signs of renewal in the Holy Spirit is a greater love for other Christians, particularly those in our congregation. Jesus stressed this when he said, 'By this will all men know that you are my disciples, if you have love for one another' (John 13: 35).

The building up of Christian fellowship in congregations

depends on our willingness to let the Lord handle the disagreements that arise among us. Wherever we are – in a house group, in a parochial committee, in a local council of churches, in a denominational synod – we find other Christians who have differences of opinion and varying concerns in their faith and practice. These differences can stretch from trivial matters, like what colour the church hall should be painted, to more serious affairs, such as our attitude as a congregation towards a campaign for unilateral nuclear disarmament in the neighbourhood.

In our age the media has encouraged confrontational methods of settling differences. Politicians, experts, commentators and ordinary people are ranged against one another in print, on the radio and on TV, with the object of defeating the other's views by skilful debate or majority votes. Unfortunately these confrontational methods have tended to spill over into the Church. Often the impression is given that the debate has more to do with entertainment than with seeking the truth.

But the Christian disciple has to learn that differences between us must be dealt with in Jesus' way, not the world's. Christ did not try to force his teaching on anyone, nor did he shout them down. He presented his teaching with authority; he pointed his hearers towards the will of his Father and explained what it meant to believe, to repent, to love and to serve the Gospel. But men and women were left free to accept or reject his teaching.

Others must be respected for their convictions. There are certain fundamental Christian truths, revealed in the scriptures and summarised in the creed, which are the framework within which we believe and live as a community of the Lord; but beyond that framework there are teachings and practices about which we can justly differ because we are not yet agreed on what God's will is for them. It is very unusual for the one we disagree with to be totally opposed to God and for us to be totally within his will!

Differences between Christians are like the oscillations of

a compass needle. The pointer swings from one extreme to another: the true direction is somewhere in between those extremes. So we should beware of condemning those with whom we disagree. 'Judge not that you be not judged' (Matt. 7: 1).

Yet even if we respect the convictions of others, that doesn't mean that our own convictions are purely personal matters. We don't always have a right to say and do just what we like. We are not independent in these things. We are responsible to God and to others in the Church. Our convictions will influence others for bad as well as for good, and that is something we have to reckon with. Otherwise we shall be treating others as if we are saying, 'I have no need of you' (1 Cor. 12: 21).

The parish church of which I am a member has had to face a common problem. What to do with a Victorian building which requires much alteration if it is to be worth restoring? Suggestions about restructuring the interior to provide meeting rooms and a kitchen caused distress among older members of the congregation, who loved the building for all that it meant to them and their families in the past fifty, sixty and even seventy years. A lot of emotion is associated with the place where your parents were married, your children were baptised, and from which the departed members of your family were buried.

The rector wisely gave the congregation two years to think and pray about the problem and organised times of intercession for God's guidance. Various ideas were presented and discussed; some were discarded. Members of the parochial church council and others visited other churches where similar restructuring had taken place. There was much circulation of notes and drawings among everybody.

Eventually a set of plans was produced and presented to the congregation with slides and a commentary. After inviting comments, the parochial church council accepted the plans unanimously and the work was put in hand with a sense of expectancy among the congregation that the Lord was providing them with a new opportunity in their neighbourhood.

The fruit of patience was a key to the process of decision-making. Everyone was made to feel that there was no rush, that what mattered was to seek God's will, not to give in to deep-seated prejudices. Time meant that those with doubts and anxieties had a chance to examine the roots of them without feeling they were being pressurised. Gradually they came to set the interests of the congregation and the mission of the Church first in their considerations as they realised the possibilities that were being presented.

In ecumenical gatherings it is often discovered that we are closer to someone in another congregation over a certain issue than a member of our own church. Debates about moral issues, for example, find us in alliance with a Roman Catholic or a Methodist against a fellow Anglican, and so on. Similarly with discussions about church order or evangelistic strategy. The experience reminds us of the unpredictability of the Holy Spirit. Christians travel by different paths to reach the same goal, although the way must always be Christ's.

'Let us then pursue what makes for peace and for mutual upbuilding,' wrote Paul to the Church in Rome (Rom. 14: 19). It is a good text to produce at the beginning of any church meeting!

Sometimes differences have to be brought out into the open and faced together. We don't like doing this. The experience can be painful – at least, initially. And it can cause tempers to rise. But the result is always cleansing – provided those who engage in it are prepared to wait for God to deal with the situation.

I realised the grace that can be given through such reconciliations in an incident that occurred while I was at Whatcombe House. It happened during one particular week when, at the end of a series of tiring conferences, the members of the community were feeling particularly frustrated with one another. Misunderstandings had arisen; grievances abounded among us.

On the Wednesday morning we gathered as usual in the little chapel for the community eucharist, the warden presiding. We struggled through the first part of the service in a flat, unenthusiastic atmosphere.

Then, when we came to the general confession, one of the members suddenly burst out, 'I can't go on with this! I don't feel I can receive Communion with you!'

Several others murmured their agreement.

The warden thought for a moment.

'We'll stop the service here,' he said, 'and do our jobs round the house this morning. Then we'll have a community meeting after lunch to talk about it.'

We left the chapel with mingled feelings of relief and apprehension.

I was glad to be away from the house that morning – sitting on the tractor mowing the lawns. Lunch was a tense experience. At two o'clock we gathered for a long community meeting. Hurt feelings were expressed. There was much frank speaking.

Then things changed. Misunderstandings were being cleared up. Others' viewpoints were being accepted. By tea-time the sense of forgiveness and unity was strong among us.

'Shall we go back into the chapel and finish the eucharist?' asked the warden.

We said we'd like to do that. Back to the chapel we went. The bread and the wine were still on the table; our books were still open on the seats where we'd left them. It was as if the Lord was saying to us, 'Everything is ready, come to my Supper.'

The words of the general confession and absolution meant more to me that afternoon than at any other time I can remember! So, too, did the giving of the peace. How we hugged one another!

Of course, in a large congregation it is not possible to achieve the same degree of intimacy as in a small community

– at least, not with every member of it. But the need for
forgiveness and reconciliation is no less because of that. We
cannot expect to be reconciled to God in Christ if we are not
also working for reconciliation among ourselves as well.

Our relationships with the Christian fellowship are rarely
confined to one congregation or group. Through the
decision-making structures of our denominations we form
links with other local churches. We join societies and
organisations that bring us together with other Christians.
Through local councils of churches with their prayer-groups
and committees we find ourselves drawn towards members
of other denominations. At college or at work we attend
Christian gatherings of believers from a wide geographical
area.

What is known as dual membership has been a feature of
denominational and ecumenical life for a long time. For
some years the Church of England has recognised the right
of its members to be on the electoral role of two different
parishes. This was to allow its members to be involved in
parochial church councils where they lived and also where
they spent a proportion of their time elsewhere (at work, at
college, at leisure).

But dual membership can drag us into conflicting
loyalties. Let me outline a situation which is not uncommon
these days.

We go to our local church regularly and we serve on one
or two of its committees; the members of our family are
linked with its organisations. We know most of the
congregation, by sight if not all by name, and we are close
friends with three or four of its members.

In the last year or so, we have become involved in a
prayer-group which meets in another part of the town. It is
led by a married couple who are not themselves attached to
any congregation; they believe that God has called them to
act as informal pastors to this particular group, and this they
do very well, for they have spiritual gifts that equip them to

care for and teach others.

We learn much from this group, we receive help from its members during a personal crisis, and we find a new freedom in the Holy Spirit through its fellowship, especially in spontaneous prayer and in ministry to one another through the laying-on of hands.

Soon we begin to feel a tension between belonging to the local church and belonging to the prayer-group. The local church seems set in its ways, unchanging in its formal worship and unresponsive to new ideas. In the prayer-group spiritual gifts like speaking in tongues and prophecies are encouraged and there is a high degree of commitment among its members.

Gradually, belonging to the prayer-group makes more and more demands on our time. We have to choose between a meeting of a local church committee and a meeting of the prayer-group. We feel torn in different directions. Other members of the prayer-group feel this, too. They begin to talk about leaving their local churches and making the prayer-group their basic Christian community. What should we do?

In matters of dual membership like this (and this applies to many different situations) we have to discern where our *primary* loyalty lies. And this we can only do in the light of our *overall* Christian discipleship, not just in response to our personal needs at a particular moment.

What I mean is this. A small group of Christians can offer one another powerful personal support. That is why in congregations nowadays house groups and similar gatherings are encouraged, to strengthen the fellowship of the congregation and to encourage initiatives in service and evangelism. But when such a group is independent, when it has no meaningful links with any wider body of Christians, then its members' opportunity for exercising a wider discipleship is seriously impeded.

It's not easy to demonstrate this to Christians whose only experience of the Church is in one local congregation. Why can't independent congregations just be linked together through informal friendships and make a united witness in the town or the city in that way?

The fact is that informal links through friendships just won't do. The commitment of Christians to one another in the Lord is more than being friendly. Wider relationships have to be undergirded by specific commitments and decision-making structures, otherwise they fade away when local leaders are less friendly with one another. The history of independency in Britain is a lesson in this.

The ministry exercised through the spiritual gift of oversight (*episcope*) is necessary if congregations are to be held together. How that oversight is exercised is a matter of historical development and theological insight. It can vary from the corporate oversight of a Methodist Conference to the personal oversight of an Anglican or Roman Catholic bishop. Without it individual congregations have great difficulty in initiating and sustaining ministries in areas where there is little local support.

Ecumenical bodies like the British Council of Churches try to help the denominations to exercise an oversight together nationally, and partnership with Christians overseas requires international structures like the Vatican or the Lambeth Conferences and the Anglican Consultative Council.

Since I came to Manchester in 1975 my ministry as an ecumenical officer has taken me into all kinds of Christian gatherings – prayer-groups and house churches, denominational congregations and religious communities, ecclesiastical synods and councils of churches. Often I have been struck by the enthusiasm of the smaller, independent groups and contrasted them with the slowness of the larger, denominational bodies. It would be all too easy to assume that the Holy Spirit was active in the former and stifled in the latter!

But that would be to grieve the Spirit. For all their vitality, independent groups have grave weaknesses. So much depends on the charismatic leadership of one or two members. They are prone to divisiveness. They tend to be authoritarian. They are out of touch with so much that God is doing in the wider Christian fellowship. Their united witness is haphazard and fickle. Although they often enjoy a deep relationship among their members, they are paralysed when they try to launch out into a wider ministry.

The larger, denominational bodies, on the other hand, have resources which enable them to make decisions together and to initiate and sustain new work in areas like the inner city and the new housing estate where independent groups are noticeably absent. They can also provide specialist ministries in sectors of society which independent Christian bodies usually ignore – industry, community relations, the media, colleges of further education. And their individual congregations can taste the renewing power of the Holy Spirit through charismatic leaders and develop their Christian witness through the denominational and ecumenical networks to which they belong.

These, then, are matters which we should consider when we discern where our primary loyalty lies for our overall Christian discipleship. If discipleship involves more than my immediate circle of Christian friends, if it involves me with Christians in other towns, cities, counties throughout the nation, and with Christians in other countries, then I have to take into account my commitment to the wider Church.

Now I'm not saying independent groups shouldn't exist! Often they have been formed because of the failure of the denominational congregations in a locality to be the Church in that place. We can learn much from them. We can be blessed by their fellowship. We can co-operate with them in ministry and mission, if they are willing to join with us. But we should know to whom our primary loyalty is due.

However, there will be times when we change our primary loyalties from one congregation to another.

One such occasion may be as a result of pastoral policy. Strong congregations sometimes encourage a few of their members to join another, weaker church, to assist it in its growth and mission. If we are involved with such a move, we should be sure to do it with the prayers and goodwill of all concerned.

It is a stimulus to our Christian life to be involved in a new work, especially if it means being part of a congregation which has small beginnings. We discover that God gives us fresh spiritual power to undertake new tasks for him.

Another reason for changing churches is when the life of our congregation seems to die or when its character changes drastically, perhaps through alterations in the pastoral leadership. We no longer feel at home in it as we once did; we sense a spiritual vacuum in the midst of its membership.

Should we always remain loyal to a congregation, whatever happens? Is it always our duty to hang on, praying and hoping that the Spirit will renew its members in their first love?

At one time I would have said, yes. Now I'm not so sure. There are circumstances when hanging on can have a corrosive effect on our own faith. For example, in times of personal need, it can be dreadfully discouraging if you seek the grace of God among your congregation and fail to find it there.

And for Christian families, the issue can be critical.

A friend of mine, an Anglican clergyman, was appointed to a post with a Church organisation in London. This meant that he had to live with his family in what Anglican clergymen usually call, 'somebody else's parish'. In these circumstances Anglican clergymen are usually expected to attach themselves to their parish church, and this is what my friend did. He went to it regularly with his wife and teenage children and occasionally helped in the services.

Within a few months it became evident there was little attempt in that church to build up the fellowship of the congregation through prayer and ministry to one another. People went to church, attended the parochial church council, and supported functions like whist-drives and jumble sales. The worship was conducted as if it was little more than a weary routine.

My friend's family revolted. They were not going to that church any more, they said. Attempts to persuade them made Sunday mornings a miserable time. Eventually, the teenagers found Christian friends among the youth club of a near-by Baptist congregation and began attending that church on Sundays.

Had my friend been a layman it wouldn't have raised much comment. But because he was an ordained priest of the Church of England, it was a cause of embarrassment. Anglican clergymen are not usually expected to attend Baptist churches! Fortunately his bishop was an understanding person and did not allow the situation to affect my friend's work.

Yet another reason for leaving our congregation is when we move our home. Sometimes it may be possible to continue attending the same church, but if this means a lengthy journey by car or public transport, that is unsatisfactory. Our links with the congregation are bound to weaken. Furthermore, there is much to be said for the Christians in a neighbourhood going to the same church. In this way they get to know one another and become a more effective witness to those among whom they live.

When we move to another house, then, we are faced with the problem, Which church should we go to? The answer, of course, is, the church the Lord wants us to join. Congregations are his creation. If we are not in the congregation where he intends us to be, we shall be hindered from fulfilling our discipleship.

This is such an important matter that we ought to look at it in more detail.

The Lord's choice of a congregation for us will be determined by what he knows about us and what his purposes are for that congregation. He knows that, as individuals and as families, we need others to support us in

our discipleship, to advise us and to teach us, to correct us
and to encourage us. He also knows that the spiritual gifts he
bestows on us are needed by that congregation in order that
they may fulfil his mission.

So pray expecting God to reveal his choice to you and to
your family or to the people you share your life with.
Although some inter-church families have to divide
themselves between two different congregations for a time,
it is obviously best if all go to the same church. So shop
around for a few weeks. There's nothing wrong in visiting
different churches, although remember there are many parts
of the world where Christians only have one choice – and
sometimes none at all!

Eventually you will together feel drawn to one particular
church. Set yourself the objective of attending it for six
months. Go on weekdays as well as on Sundays to get to
know the members and to become known by them. Invite
some of them round to your house. Don't try to get to know
everybody. That will be exhausting, unless the membership
is very small. Believe the Lord will show you the individuals
and families he wants you to meet.

Make a point of meeting the pastoral leadership during
these first weeks (the parish priest and the church-wardens,
or the minister and the elders, or the pastor and the
deacons). This will help you to understand what vision they
have for the church. Is this a vision God wants you to be
identified with?

If there are prayer or Bible groups, join one. But be
humble about it when you attend. You may feel you're God's
gift to that group, but they've got to discern that truth as well
before you can all be sure! Join in the humdrum, ordinary
jobs, like cleaning the church: this will show the congregation you want to be involved in all aspects of their life
and share in the responsibility.

Don't expect to be invited to preach because you were a
reader or local preacher in your last church. Pray that God
will help you to see what his purpose is for you in that

congregation and that they will encourage you to fulfil it among them.

And be teachable! Customs vary in different churches. If the worship is different from what happened in your last church, don't go round saying how much better things were there! Try to enter into the corporate spirit of the congregation and to appreciate what it offers you before you start making suggestions.

When the six months are over, make an appointment to have a private talk with the clergy or the pastoral leadership to discuss what is involved in joining the congregation and what your ministry should be in it. Don't expect the minister to accept without question all that you put before him. You may have a conviction that God is calling you to a particular task in the fellowship: the minister may know the rest of the congregation have not discerned that spiritual gift in you yet! There are plenty of ways of serving a congregation while you wait for them to discern the task you have set your heart on and so confirm your conviction of God's purpose for you among them.

It is usually beneficial to belong to a group in the congregation – a prayer-group, a Bible-study group, or something of the sort. The more intimate fellowship of six, eight or ten believers is a strong foundation for Christian discipleship. We can share with them, ask them to pray for specific concerns, learn more of our faith together, and initiate acts of service and mission in the neighbourhood.

But it is not always possible to be a member of such a group at certain times. Family responsibilities, work programmes and other factors make that kind of commitment difficult. Then we have to be content with a more informal grouping among the members of the congregation.

Be careful you don't find yourself running round too many committees so that you have no time to do anything in depth. There's a lot to be done in a local church and it's very easy for a willing member to be overworked if he or she is anxious to please. Don't be too available to everybody.

Make sure that what you do is what the Lord wants you to do, not what other people want you to do. To be so involved in the congregation's affairs that we have little time or energy for our families or for other things in life is disastrous.

Too often Christians assume that to be active in and around the local church is the essence of discipleship. That can be a grave error. God calls us into the Church to serve him in his world – the world he sent his Son to save. For us the world begins with our families and the people among whom we live and stretches out from our places of work and leisure to society in general and social needs in particular.

We shall explore this aspect of discipleship later.

CHAPTER 7

Called and Sent

In the last chapter I discussed our membership of the local church, our primary loyalties in the midst of rival demands made on us by different Christian communities, and our need for discernment in joining a new congregation. Now I want to consider the role of the local church in our Christian discipleship.

I've often revolted against the expression, 'going to church'. It seems to me to emphasise the wrong things about being a Christian – that the Church is a building (when what Christians should be concerned about is *being the Church* in the world), that what matters most is being present at an act of worship (when what Christians should be concerned about is relating their worship to their life), and so on.

But if we interpret 'going to church' as 'going to meet Jesus Christ in his Body, the Church', then the expression still has its uses.

Let me explain. In the New Testament disciples are those who respond to Jesus' call and who are then sent out by him to fulfil his purposes. This is what being a follower of Christ was all about.

Jesus called people. He invited those burdened with sin to come to him for forgiveness. He summoned individuals like Simon Peter and Andrew to come to him for particular tasks.

Others were called – that is, felt drawn to him – because they realised they needed him. Nicodemus, the woman with the issue of blood, and the rich young ruler were just three of the many who, we would say, were moved by the Holy Spirit to come to Jesus. Some were called to him through friends and relatives. Andrew brought his brother, Philip, and four men carried their paralysed companion on a stretcher to him. But however they approached him, Jesus reached out to these people and met their need – or offered to do so – in teaching, in healing, in pronouncing sins forgiven, in strengthening.

Then he sent them away. Some he sent on missions in his name; they were the 'sent-away ones', the apostles. Others left him believing him to be the Messiah and to thank God for him through changed lives. Nicodemus went back with much to think about, the woman with the issue of blood left him joyfully healed, the rich young ruler departed with a heavy heart unable to accept his word.

This pattern of discipleship – of being called by Jesus and of being sent away by him – continued after the resurrection, but with a new dynamism, since the followers of Christ realised that the risen Lord was now with them by his Spirit. His presence was especially manifested when they assembled in his name.

In the book of Acts the calling and the sending of the disciples was intimately linked with the assembly of God's people. Jesus spoke directly to Peter on the roof-top in Joppa, and to Paul on the road to Damascus; but their response to him involved them with other members of the Church, who also had to hear (that is, discern) the Lord's word to them.

Philip was sent to work in Samaria, but his mission had to be inspected by the Church in Jerusalem, who sent down Peter and John for that purpose. Similarly, Peter's striking initiative in baptising the Gentile household of Cornelius in response to Christ's call had to be accepted by the Church in Jerusalem meeting under the presidency of James. So, in the sense in which I have expounded the phrase, it was in 'going to Church' that 'with great power the apostles gave their testimony to the resurrection of the Lord Jesus, and great grace was upon them all' (Acts 4: 33).

And so it should be today. Our local congregation should be a special sign of Christ's presence in our lives. Our discipleship should be related to coming to him in that congregation and in being sent out by him from them.

Like those who came to Jesus during his earthly ministry, we gather as Christians in groups and in congregations for a variety of reasons – for forgiveness, for healing, for fellowship, for guidance, for strengthening in the face of decisions or tensions in our lives. We sense the inner compulsion of the Holy Spirit to assemble in Jesus' name.

When we come together, we also come into the presence of Christ. It is the love of God as manifested in the attitude of church members to one another which reveals Jesus most powerfully. The new commandment our Lord gave his disciples was that they should love one another, and this injunction is echoed again and again in the epistles: 'May the Lord make you increase and abound in love to one another and to all men' (1 Thess. 3. 12); 'Let brotherly love continue' (Heb. 13: 1); 'Love one another earnestly from the heart' (1 Pet. 1: 22); 'Let us love one another, for love is of God, and he who loves is born of God and knows God' (1 John 4: 7).

Through worship and fellowship, through teaching and discussions, through ministering to one another and accepting responsibility for one another, we find Christ in the local church, meeting our needs, forgiving us, healing us, guiding us and strengthening us.

In the Christian fellowship we also discover our weaknesses. I have been in a prayer-group where the love of God among those present has been so powerful that I have been jolted into realising my own lukewarmness. I have been with two or three others in some joint project when their discernment and boldness in the Holy Spirit has shamed me for my blindness and timidity.

'Going to Church' in this way also shows openly that we want to make ourselves available to Jesus Christ within the Christian community. We offer ourselves to him in the company of his people to be equipped by the Holy Spirit as his disciples. In recent years, especially through the influence of the charismatic movement, we have been given a fresh understanding of the Spirit's gifts. We are learning again from the scriptures to expect Jesus to anoint us with his power and to exercise charisms in ministry to others.

'As each has received a gift, employ it for one another, as good stewards of God's varied grace: whoever speaks, as one who utters oracles of God; whoever renders service, as one who renders it by the strength which God supplies; in order that in everything God may be glorified through Jesus Christ' (1 Pet. 4: 10–11).

For teaching about spiritual gifts, this passage is a little gem. *Each* has a charism: no one is excluded. Gifts are employed for *one another*: they are not endowments of grace for the sole benefit of the one who exercises them. *Stewards* are authorised persons who are responsible for their master's property: what they handle is not their own. God's grace is *varied*: he shows his love and power in different ways through different people. Some gifts attract attention, like speaking God's *oracles* in prophecy or inspired teaching; other gifts, like *service*, are ordinary, even humdrum. Nevertheless, both the spectacular and the ordinary charisms are exercised *by the strength* which God supplies. And all gifts are used in what we say or do *in order that in everything God may be glorified through Jesus Christ*. If we are orientated to the Spirit, our ministry will point to the Lord rather than to ourselves.

Being a disciple of Jesus Christ, then, involves us with other Christians because it is together that we fulfil his ministry by the Spirit in the world. As Christ's human body was an expression of the Spirit's activity in his incarnate life, so our human bodies are to express unitedly the activity of the same Spirit now.

It was in the power of the Spirit that Jesus fulfilled his Father's will. He was 'the anointed One', the *Christos*, anointed by the Spirit at his baptism. His whole ministry from his temptations in the wilderness to his death on the cross was a demonstration of the Spirit's power. His life and his death were, in the fullest sense of the word, charismatic. It would be an interesting exercise to work through the Gospel narratives and list the spiritual gifts which Jesus exercised: teaching, prophecy, words of wisdom and knowledge, discernment, exorcism, healing, leadership, celibacy, martyrdom.

When we come to him in the Church, he equips us with charisms to fulfil his ministry alongside his other disciples. The title, 'the body of Christ', is particularly evocative when we think of the gifts which we exercise corporately with all Christians in his name. It was in the context of teaching about spiritual gifts that Paul said to the Corinthian Church, 'Now you are the body of Christ and individually members of it' (1 Cor. 12: 27).

Like the first disciples, we need to be equipped before Jesus sends us out.

Before we discuss spiritual gifts any further, though, we ought to think for a moment of what Jesus is equipping us for. The usual reply in charismatic circles is to say that we are being built up 'for the common good' (1 Cor. 12: 7) and 'for ... the body of Christ' (Eph. 4: 12).

This is, of course, true as far as it goes, but in some discussions it doesn't go far enough. For although the epistles are concerned about the Christian fellowship because it was matters arising from local congregations that caused them to be written, it is in the teaching of Jesus that disciples were called and sent out for the kingdom of God.

Jesus said remarkably little about the Church as such (although he said a good deal about relationships between his disciples and their ministry in the world). In fact, the word itself is only used twice: once in Matthew 16: 18, where Jesus responded to Peter's confession of faith by saying it was on such a rock that he would build his Church, and once in Matthew 18: 17, where he directed that faults between disciples should be confessed to the Church if they could not be settled privately.

What was central to Christ's teaching was the immanence of the kingdom of God. 'The time is fulfilled, and the kingdom of God is at hand; repent, and believe in the gospel' (Mark 1: 15). That kingdom was present in the person of Jesus himself, manifested in his complete obedience to his Father. The disciples would see the kingdom breaking through into this world wherever men and women were similarly obedient to God. The disciples were exhorted to seek it for themselves above all else: 'But seek first his kingdom and his righteousness' (Matt. 6: 33).

Yet the kingdom had an elusive quality. Men would seek it, but make mistakes in discerning its presence. It would not be established in its fullness until the end of the age. What is experienced of the kingdom in this life is but a foretaste of what is to come. Hence the disciples are to be watchful for its final coming. 'Your kingdom come' is to be their daily prayer.

With what might be called a kingdom-goal to our discipleship, we are steered away from being over-preoccupied with a church-goal. In our congregations we tend to concentrate our attention on our life together, our worship, our buildings, our traditions and our programmes. We find it easier to busy ourselves with our own affairs rather than with the affairs of the neighbourhood within which we live. In the theological jargon of today, we become more concerned with maintenance than with mission.

The kingdom-goal reminds us that Jesus requires of his disciples more than just faithful church membership. Being his disciple means responding to his Gospel of the kingdom and following him into his world. We do not belong to the Church for our own sake, or for the sake of the Church, but for the sake of the kingdom. Our conversion is for the kingdom. Our personal growth in the Spirit is for the kingdom. Our fellowship in the Church is for the kingdom. Our spiritual gifts are for the kingdom.

In anything that we think, say or do, a key to following the Holy Spirit is to find the right answer to the question, Will it affirm the kingdom of God?

Of course, the fellowship and upbuilding of the Church in the local congregation is vital. It isn't even secondary. It's one with seeking the kingdom. Our unity with the Church is the means through which we respond to the Gospel. Without the worship and reflection, the encouragement and discernment provided by the Christian community, we should flounder, maybe doing all sorts of good works but drifting away from God.

But we must always be looking beyond the Church to the Gospel of the kingdom for which we exist. That's what it means to have a kingdom-goal to our discipleship.

People come to me and say something like this: 'It's all very well telling us what the New Testament says about spiritual gifts, but how am I to know what my spiritual gifts are? I can't be fulfilling my ministry because I haven't a clue what the Holy Spirit wants to do through me!'

The first thing I advise them is to stop thinking about their ministry. Seek first the kingdom of God. Spiritual gifts are about God's work, not ours; and if we spend time wondering whether this charism or that is ours, we shall be so concerned about ourselves that we shall miss the Lord's leading in our lives.

The second thing I advise them is to offer to God the things that they can do. Our natural abilities and interests are often tools that God uses. What do we like doing? What do others tell us they appreciate about the things we do or say? Instead of looking for gifts of healing or prophecy, let's start with the gifts we have now. It'll be time to seek higher gifts when we are aware of God's power in ordinary encounters and tasks.

When I was a parish priest there was a man in the congregation who was not very comfortable in the sort of activities that congregations engage in – prayer-groups, committees, taking part in services, witnessing, and so on.

But he was a wonderful gardener. After he was converted, he gave several hours each week to the grounds round the church. Within a year or two the lawns, flowers, shrubs and paths were beautiful. People stopped to admire them. Some chatted with him. Yes, he used to tell them, he went to this church. Yes, he believed in God. Yes, he had given his life to Jesus Christ. And the grass? Well, it was rather heavy soil, but he had tried a new fertiliser on it this year and ...

He could never have stood on a box in the grounds and preached, but his natural gift, offered for the glory of God, was used to proclaim the Gospel in another way.

Changes in our circumstances can open up new gifts for us. A Christian woman who was left a widow felt impelled, a few years after her husband's death, to spend more time in prayer. She got up earlier, read books, used the liturgy of the hours, went on retreats. Gradually she was able to put aside three hours for prayer each day, in spite of a busy job. Her intercessions for the congregation, for her neighbours, and for individuals became a valued ministry.

We often discover spiritual gifts through new opportunities that the Lord gives us. A young married couple moved into the district and joined a local church. Within a short time they found other young people talking to them and confiding in them about personal difficulties. At first, they were startled. In their previous local church they had been youth-club leaders. Now in a new congregation a new ministry was given them. They went on a course for counsellors in order to be better equipped.

Ministries have to be tested. Not long ago I asked for my ministry, as an ecumenical office, to be evaluated (the current in-word for testing). Three experts spent two days with me and presented a report to the council which employs me. Although it was a rather unnerving experience – I'm not used to being interrogated and my letters and files being critically (if kindly) scrutinised – I was grateful for what the evaluators did. They made several suggestions which I've found extremely helpful.

This is, perhaps, a rather formal example of testing, but anyone who exercises a ministry should be prepared for a simple evaluation occasionally. And we should be prepared to accept the fact that we may be asked to lay that ministry down. The mission of the Church is sadly hampered when members hang on to offices and tasks because no one has suggested that their effectiveness has died.

Before we can engage in ministry for the kingdom, we usually need training. Spiritual gifts require encouragement and guidance from others in the congregation or from those in the wider Church with specialist knowledge and experience. I have just mentioned the couple who went on a course on counselling so that they would be better equipped for the ministry they were being led into. They were wise. They didn't assume the Lord had given the ministry to them on a plate, as it were. They realised they had to listen to him through the educational facilities available to them.

Much damage can be caused by individuals or groups who assume that, because they have once or twice exercised a spiritual gift like healing, they are now equipped to follow that ministry anywhere with anyone. We need to submit to the pastoral leadership of the Church and accept advice about further training and experience. The gifts of the Spirit have much to do with the education we can receive from the Church and from other sources. That is why others are anointed as teachers and leaders – to teach and to lead us.

For the rest of this chapter, then, I want to outline the form of Christian education needed if we are to serve the kingdom of God when we are sent out by Jesus Christ.

Hearing the Word of the Lord is the heart-beat of all Christian education. And an important preliminary to this is becoming familiar with the text of the Bible itself. The scriptures are presented to us ritually in church services, when the reader finishes the passage by saying, 'This is the Word of the Lord.' Our response to that, 'Thanks be to God', or 'Praise to Christ our Lord', indicates we are longing to embrace that Word and to shape our lives accordingly.

In a pre-literary age, Christians learned passages of the scriptures by heart and meditated on biblical scenes depicted in stained-glass windows, murals and plays. Nowadays we have an array of educational tools to assist us – modern translations of the Bible, introductions and commentaries, daily scripture reading notes and workbooks, cassettes and video tapes. The stream of books about the Bible pouring from the publishing houses never seems to abate!

But none of these educational tools can be a substitute for reading the Bible itself. Begin with one book, or part of a book, and go through it chapter by chapter, with a commentary or some other aid beside you. Take a gospel first, then an epistle, and then a book from the Old Testament. Seek advice on how to do this.

You'll come across the problems that biblical scholars raise. Who was the author of the book? What was the cultural, social, political and religious environment in which it was written? What are the sources behind it? How does it handle the great theological themes of the faith? What is unique about its teaching? How has it been interpreted?

If this approach to the scriptures appeals to you, you might consider enrolling for a course under a competent tutor. Theological education by extension is widely available through the extramural departments of universities, Christian institutes, and the educational departments of the denominations.

But don't get so carried away by biblical scholarship that you cease to listen to the Word of God. Some people play around with Bible study rather as others play around with crossword puzzles. The object is for us to surrender our inquisitive authority over the text to the Holy Spirit and submit to his authority as he reveals its meaning to us.

Besides getting to know our way round the Bible, we need also to become familiar with the basics of Christian doctrine and ethics. Doctrine helps us to understand how the love of God reaches out to us through the incarnation of Jesus

Christ and the gift of the Holy Spirit. Ethics helps us to understand how we accept and respond to the love of God in our lives and in our relationships.

Again, you'll come across problems. How do we discern when God is speaking to us? How do we interpret the central doctrines of the Christian faith in the light of modern knowledge? How do we explain the uniqueness of the Gospel in a multi-faith society? How do we decide what is morally right in a secular age? How do we promote what is good and reject what is evil in a rapidly advancing technological world? And, again, we mustn't be so carried away by the fascination of the problems that we miss the guidance of the Holy Spirit.

Beyond these basic subjects, the field of Christian education stretches away to wide horizons. Everything in human life has some bearing on Christian discipleship. Opportunities for specialisation are everywhere, when we feel God is leading us that way.

There's much to be said for learning something of the Christian traditions through which we have come to faith in Jesus Christ. We need to know our apostolic roots if we are to be a prophetic Church.

In the summer of 1983 I attended a conference at Keble College, Oxford, organised to celebrate the 150th anniversary of the Oxford Movement. I have already described my early upbringing in the Anglo-Catholic tradition of the Church of England. That tradition, with its stress on the sacramental means of grace and the office of the ordained ministry, received a fresh impetus in the 1830s through the teaching and writing of three Oxford dons, John Henry Newman, John Keble and Edward Bouverie Pusey. The conference explored various aspects of their contribution to the Church of England.

It was a fascinating week: daily worship in the chapel of Keble College; lectures and discussions; a tour of Newman's rooms in Oriel College and in the little community house he founded at Littlemore; an exhibition of manuscripts at the

Bodleian Library; a display of old vestments from the days of the ritualist troubles; and a sermon by Bishop Trevor Huddleston in St Mary's University Church exactly 150 years (to the day and the hour) since John Keble's sermon on what he called 'the national apostasy', which is regarded as the beginning of the Oxford Movement.

Like some Anglican high churchmen, I've tended to be critical of some contemporary manifestations of Anglo-Catholicism – opposition to the ordination of women, objections to schemes for the reunion of the Church – and found it difficult to identify with what is almost a cult of the ordained ministry among some of its adherents. Yet the week left me with a profound sense of the continuity of God's grace among his people. The Oxford Movement was a fresh breath of the Holy Spirit sweeping over the Anglican Communion recalling her to greater holiness of life and greater faithfulness in mission. And I was grateful to be reminded of that.

For the same reason, there's much to be said for learning something of other Christian traditions. What has God to say to us through Evangelical, Pentecostal, Radical, Roman Catholic, Orthodox, Baptist, and all the other streams of Christian spirituality? Through local councils of churches and ecumenical groups we shall find our discipleship enriched by what we learn from them.

Go back to the church where you were baptised and/or confirmed and reflect on what Christian initiation means to you now. Go back to the church where you were converted, healed, married, ordained, or whatever, and examine where God has led you during the intervening years. These memories are precious when we assess our discipleship today and thank the Lord for his faithfulness.

The lives of other Christians can encourage us. Paper-backed biographies of men and women who have been used by the Holy Spirit are published by the hundreds of thousands these days. Reviewers of books in church papers tend to be dismissive of them, with disparaging remarks about 'charismatic success stories'. Well, perhaps that kind of criticism is occasionally justified. But it has to be weighed against the enormous teaching value of such books. Here is a way of 'doing theology' through the stories of others' experiences of God's grace.

Jesus taught in parables. His stories drew on the experience, imagination and judgment of his listeners. Popular books of this kind can do something similar. We can see how our contemporaries rely on prayer, fellowship, spiritual gifts, and learn from them.

This is especially true of those stories which have come down to us from previous centuries. Think how the lives of people like Francis of Assisi, John Wesley and Hudson Taylor (to name only three among so great a cloud of witnesses) continue to inspire us today.

Some of the things I have been listing are learned formally through courses of sermons, discussion groups, directed reading and evening classes. But many other things we discover through our involvement with a local church. For example, in a congregation where members practise tithing, a newcomer will probably pick up lessons about Christian giving from his contact with others. Similarly, a local church which sets its face against any forms of racism will soon let individual members know if they have prejudices.

It is the responsibility of the pastoral leadership to see that attitudes developed among members are tested alongside the teaching of the scriptures as they are handed down in the Church. As problems and opportunities arise in the congregation, they too can be occasions of learning God's will. I illustrated this in the last chapter from the process by which a local church came to accept the need for modernising its building.

One of the most powerful learning situations is in worship. The liturgy is, of course, much more than a teaching medium. We shall explore the place of worship in our discipleship in the last chapter. But education – in the widest sense of the word – certainly happens when we assemble to praise the Lord.

The scripture readings and everything else that belongs to the ministry of the Word in the liturgy are concerned with proclaiming the Gospel of the kingdom to us. We learn, too, from the texts of prayers and hymns, inspired as they are by biblical themes and personal experiences of Christian discipleship. The sacramental signs used in worship – bread and wine, water, oil, the laying-on of hands – proclaim their own lesson about God's grace. Other rituals – processions, crosses, palms, ashes, candles, colours, vestments – contribute to our education.

The great mysteries of our faith are unfolded each year in the liturgical calendar: creation and the call of Israel in the Christmas season; the incarnation at Christmas and Epiphany; the ministry, passion, death, and resurrection of Christ in the weeks leading to Holy Week and Easter; the ascension and the gift of the Spirit at Pentecost; and the life and teaching of the apostolic Church after Pentecost.

Special occasions bring their own lessons to reinforce what we have been taught and to give us new insights. The services of Christian initiation challenge us afresh on what it means to be a follower of the Lord – especially the baptism, confirmation and first Communion of adults who affirm for themselves their repentance and faith. Prayers of thanksgiving for the birth or for the adoption of a child convey a powerful sense of sharing in the responsibility of God's creation and the purposes of the family. So does a marriage. Services of prayer for healing help us not only to seek a gift of the Spirit but also to reflect on what it means to participate in the passion of Christ through the sufferings of this world. The funeral service before the burial of one of the congregation brings that mixture of sadness at the loss of a loved friend and of joy at the hope promised in the resurrection of Jesus.

Saints' days and holy days, feasts of the dedication of the church building, harvest thanksgivings, covenant services and stewardship Sundays – these and other celebrations remind us of various aspects of discipleship in the Church and in the world.

Sometime after the exile in Babylon, perhaps during the fourth and the third centuries B.C., the scribes of Israel began to collect together all the sayings which had been handed down by earlier teachers on what was deemed necessary for a godly life. This collection is known to students of the Bible as 'wisdom literature' because much of it was traditionally ascribed to Solomon, a man wise in the ways of God.

A key verse in this literature is, 'The fear of the Lord is the beginning of knowledge' (Prov. 1: 7); it appears over and over again, and is repeated in worship (e.g., Psalm 111: 10). By 'fear' is meant the loving yet awesome reverence at the presence of the living God in the midst of such instruction.

This prepared the way for the New Testament realisation that the Christian's teacher is not a wise man but God himself, the Holy Spirit, who speaks and demonstrates the Word though those whom he anoints for that purpose.

In Christian education, then, our teacher is the Holy Spirit. He is the one who guides us (which is what 'to educate' means). As we become more orientated towards him, we shall recognise his presence in the people and things and events that teach us and hear God's Word through them. We shall also learn how to be used as a teacher of that Word through his power.

While I was in Oxford at the conference, I bought a copy of Pusey's *Parochial Sermons* in two nice leather-bound volumes. In one of these, entitled 'The Teaching of God within and without', Dr Pusey took as his text, 'The secret of the Lord is with them that fear him, and he will shew them his covenant' (Ps. 25: 14 AV), to demonstrate that God can teach us much from the people and events that happen around us ('without'), but his lessons do not change our lives unless we allow him to change our hearts ('within').

That is the essence of Christian education. That is what happens when Jesus Christ calls us to himself in his Church.

In Pusey's words:

> God's outward voice reveals; his inward voice applies what it has revealed. His outward voice declares what we are to believe; his inward voice opens our ears and our hearts, that we may believe and love and do. Without his inward voice, we would be like an instrument unattuned, which can give forth none but harsh and discordant sounds. Without his outward voice, we should be like the same instrument, attuned, but with none to play upon it.[1]

So, having called us and equipped us by his Word, Jesus Christ sends us out into his world.

Of course, we don't leave his presence when we leave the company of other Christians. Nor do we cease to be members of the Church when we are alone or when we are with non-Christians. But we do leave that particular manifestation of his presence to which he referred when he spoke of being with the two or the three who come together in his name.

He sends us out to fulfil the purposes of the kingdom in the power of his Holy Spirit. That is why, at the end of the eucharist, we say: Send us out in the power of your Spirit to live and work to your praise and glory.

[1] E.B. Pusey, *Parochial Sermons*, Vol. 2 (1862), p. 242.

CHAPTER 8

Citizens and Sojourners

I was at a conference on parish renewal a few years ago and heard remarkable stories of congregations coming to life in the power of the Holy Spirit.

Yet for me the most outstanding contribution was from a man who did not speak about parish renewal at all (in its narrower sense). He described what his Christian discipleship meant to him in his job.

Briefly, he said what it meant to him as head of the probation services in a local authority, in his relationships with his staff and in caring for different cases brought to him.

He concluded by saying something like this: 'Now and then I meet young men and women who've been in our care and who've settled down. They're in steady jobs and they've got homes and families of their own. When that happens, I thank God for letting me see just another sign of his kingdom breaking through into the world.'

What impressed me was the integrity of his discipleship. It was as important to him in his work as in his home.

Some Christians privatise their religion. That is to say, they regard Christian beliefs and practices as things which concern their private lives – at home and in a local church – and in their workaday world adopt the same attitudes and standards as everyone else.

Many find it difficult to see any connection between their religion and their jobs. So they make decisions and accept practices which would not be tolerated in their homes.

Others fear they will be unpopular if they make a stand for Christian principles in the protection of the weak, the unjustly treated, the sexually harassed, or the grievously treated.

This is why it is sometimes difficult to get Christians to identify themselves as a group in their places of employment. They prefer to lie low. Chaplains in universities, colleges, hospitals, industry and the armed forces complain of this reticence.

An Anglican priest, who had worked for three years in a modern university, wrote to the members of the staff with whom he had been in contact at the end of his appointment:

> There is a chronic reluctance on the part of Christians here to join in any religious activity, whoever organises it, although the place is riddled with them. No doubt they uphold the suburban captivity of the Church by filling active, probably evangelical, churches on Sundays. This represents a real failure of responsibility. There is a continual lack of co-operation among Christians, the Christian Union in particular perpetrating a ministry to a diminishing number of students in splendid isolation.
>
> But the real disappointment for me behind all this is that, if you separate out the responsibilities of a Christian minister into the roles of prophet, priest and pastor (a possible model), then there has been no lack of call on the last aspect, insufficient use of the priestly ministry (because the Christians will not meet), and little support for and even hostility for the prophetic role.
>
> Yet I would consider the prophetic role primary in a place like this. We should express concern about the quality of life, values and aims of the university, for it is to these that the Christian tradition has a richness of resource to contribute.

Since we are disciples of the kingdom of God, the Gospel has to be demonstrated in the way we live. If Christ makes all things new, then that newness has to be recognised as authentic. It is not a question of how many are converted to the Gospel through us. Rather, it is a matter of going about our daily work in a manner that allows the Holy Spirit to use us in glorifying Jesus Christ as the 'head over all things' (Eph. 1: 22). This includes our wider responsibilities as citizens in the affairs of national and international justice and peace as well.

This was expounded very powerfully in a book entitled, *The Call to Conversion*, published in 1981, stressing the need for the followers of Jesus Christ to be converted to the cause of God's kingdom in the world. It is being widely read as a remarkable contribution from an evangelical background on the need for Christian involvement in society.

The author's life-story is interesting. Jim Wallis was born in 1948 in a middle-class suburban family in Detroit. His parents were members of the conservative evangelical Plymouth Brethren Church, where his father was a senior elder. He grew up as a 'preacher's kid' and up to his teenage years he was a model son, immersed in the church, a Boy Scout leader, a good student and sportsman. But when he was about 15, he began to ask questions: 'Why did whites and blacks live in isolation from each other? Why were whites well off and blacks poor?' He was not satisfied when people in the church told him he was too young to understand, so he made his way into the black communities in inner Detroit and during his university years spent his summers in factories and on maintenance crews that were largely black. Coming to know the anger and frustration of blacks, he was saddened but not surprised when a prolonged riot (he called it an insurrection) tore Detroit apart in the mid-1960s.

He felt he had lost his faith. He threw himself into the civil rights and anti-war movements of the late 1960s. Like many of his fellow students, he demonstrated against the war in Vietnam and was gassed, roughed up and jailed by the police. 'We committed the unpardonable sin: we said that

America was wrong – wrong in the ghettos and in the jungles of South-east Asia. And for our opposition we were regarded as criminals.'

When he left university, he took a labouring job and began to read the Bible again. Jesus' teachings about the poor drew him back to faith. Matthew 25: 40, 'Truly I say to you, as you did it to one of the least of these my brethren, you did it to me,' became his 'conversion passage'. He grasped the fact that there was a sacrifical love at the heart of the Gospel which was not in the political movements he had embraced.

A lot of my Marxist friends were interested in the poor for the sake of organising them. Here was the radical value of people at the bottom for their own sake. Here was the Son of God, here was Jesus, whose natural habitation was among those at the bottom, with the suffering and the poor. To ignore and neglect and abuse them was to ignore and neglect and abuse him.

He went to Trinity Evangelical Divinity School, outside Chicago, and in 1975 moved to Washington as a pastor of the Sojourners community. This is a group of about forty people, predominantly white, middle class and university educated, who live in a poor, predominantly black neighbourhood, where many are out of work and many have lost their homes despite being in the capital of one of the world's richest nations. The community's involvement in their neighbourhood has been the inspiration of Jim Wallis's book. For them the preaching of the Gospel is not just to save souls, but to bring the kingdom of God into the world with explosive force.

Two quotations illustrate the author's vision. One reflects his evangelical stance on the necessity of conversion:

Conversion cannot be an end in itself; it is the first step of entry into the kingdom. Conversion marks the birth of the movement out of a merely private existence into a public consciousness. Conversion is the beginning of active solidarity with the purposes of the kingdom of God in the world. No longer preoccupied with our private lives, we are engaged in a vocation for the world. Our prayer becomes, 'Thy kingdom come, thy will be done, on earth as it is in heaven.' If we restrict our salvation to only inner concerns, we have yet to enter into its fullness. Turning from ourselves to Jesus identifies us with him in the world.[1]

The other illustrates his indebtedness to the Catholic concept of the Church as a living manifestation of Christ's body for God's purposes in the world:

Building the body of Christ is not one of many issues to which we are committed, as it once was; it is the basis for all that we do and all that we are. It is the environment in which and out of which we are called to live and minister in a world of pain and peril. We can confront the violence of the nuclear age only with the very life of Christ among us. We can confront the economic imperatives that lead to war only by making visible the love and simplicity that was Jesus' way of life. It is not us but his life among us that disarms the principalities and powers.[2]

Christian witness in our workaday life is usually in one of two environments.

The first is where an institution or a firm is led by Christian men and women. Some small businesses make a point of employing Christians where possible. I know of a primary school where the staff meet regularly not only to discuss school matters but also to pray together and to minister to one another. I also know of a shipping office in the City of London where the eighteen employees attend the eucharist together during their lunch-hour.

There is a school of thought which argues that a distinctly

Christian institution or firm can act as leaven in the lump of institutional and professional life: by the quality of its corporate life it witnesses to similar institutions and firms around it. Certainly some Christian schools, colleges and hospitals have this effect on similar secular establishments around them.

The other kind of environment, within which the vast majority earn their livelihood, is totally secular. I can sympathise with the individual Christian, as he or she looks round the office, shop, school, college, hospital, firm, garage, or wherever it is that he or she works, and wonders how a single person can have any influence on what happens there.

Perhaps the first step will be to look out for other Christians in the place. There may not be many, but there will almost certainly be some. Get to know them. Chat to them when opportunity arises. Sit by them in the canteen occasionally. Gently see if they have concerns about the situation. And be prepared to wait a long time for any opportunity of meeting and discussing seriously what, if anything, you should do together.

The second step is to become informed about the changes which are happening around us, especially as they affect your work. The development of communications and the crisis brought about by the advent of microtechnology, coupled with the economic recession of the last decade or so, highlights the need for the Church to seek God's guidance in helping society to adjust to these changes.

Employment is very much a Christian concern. Since the great age of industrial expansion, the Church has done much to promote the idea that paid employment is the only proper activity for man between school and retirement. The so-called 'Protestant work ethic' continues to dominate popular opinion (and therefore political policies) even though employment as we have known it is less and less available.

Previous recessions, like the one in the 1930s, affected

mainly manual and unskilled labourers and therefore not the families of those who influenced public opinion, especially Church leaders. Now it is different. The changes are having their effect on all classes of society.

A bishop, a judge and a BBC producer were talking together at a meeting and discovered that each had a child who had left university and who was unemployed.

'Only a few years ago,' said the judge, 'I'd have laughed if anyone had told me that my son, with a public school education behind him and a good degree at Cambridge, wouldn't be able to find a job.'

The other two sadly agreed with him.

The Church must engage in a prophetic ministry to support those who look to the future and see new opportunities for our society. There is a growing realisation that the worth of men and women cannot be assessed through the work they do, either in the production of goods or in service to the community.

It is being argued that all citizens have a right to a life in which their individual capabilities are trained and fulfilled whether what they do has an economic or social value or not. We must talk about activity rather than a job, about citizens' allowances rather than unemployment benefit, about an education that prepares young people for a life of varied skills rather than a job which they must compete for and hold until they retire. Work and leisure would no longer be distinct categories.

In his Reith Lectures, *On Britain* (1982), Ralf Dahrendorf, Principal of the London School of Economics, pictured a future society which for many would be a mixture of self-sufficiency, exchange and barter of goods and services, and cultural and leisure pursuits. Some would be paid, some would be unpaid, all would be underpinned by a national citizen's wage.

Community services would be developed to an extent which we only dimly see in the present welfare and job creation schemes. No stigma would be attached to an activity because it did not produce goods that can be consumed or skills that can be purchased.

It could well be that work as we know it today would only occupy part of our adult working life. Individuals would move on to other activities through job-sharing, professional-exchanges, and early 'retirement' (we would have to invent a new vocabulary for this society). It would also mean that the economy would have to be planned so that it generated sufficient funds to pay adequately for those engaged in non-productive (in the economic sense) activity.

There is much in this vision of what is called 'the service society' that echoes the hopes and prayers of Christians. A caring community, a safeguarding of the rights of the individual, an encouragement of each person's talents, a high priority to the needs of the poor, the sick, the disabled and the elderly – the picture begins to look like a secularised version of the Church herself.

What these ideas lack, of course, is commitment to the kingdom of God. Without acknowledging God as creator, the Son as redeemer, and the Holy Spirit as the one who teaches and equips, they become as empty and materialist as Marxist ideology. Outside the Gospel of the kingdom, endeavours to promote a caring community can go horribly wrong. Sin and evil gain the upper hand, selfishness replaces benevolence, greed ruins sharing, and personal ambition destroys communal service.

But here is an opportunity for Christians, individually and corporately, to become the leaven of the kingdom of God in the dough of our society. In the midst of changes we discern and support what can be truly offered to God, and we denounce and combat what is evil in them. This raises questions about our political allegiance. Can a capitalist-based philosophy promote these causes better than a socialist one?

So we look at our workday situation and seek the guidance of the Holy Spirit in fulfilling our tasks and building our relationships according to his will. People's circumstances vary so much that it is impossible to give examples that will apply to everyone. But it may well be that we shall sometime face questions like these: What do these redundancies in the department mean to me in terms of job-sharing? What opportunities are there for me to create jobs which will enable others to find greater fulfilment? If a policy is proposed which I know is evil, at what point and how do I indicate that I oppose it? In competition for promotion, am I taking an unfair advantage?

When the firm moves over to a 35-hour week, what do I do with the extra spare time? What are the needs of my neighbourhood, town or city that I should be concerned about? Is there a parents' association, a householders' association, a political party, a trade union or a professional body I should join to strengthen the Christian voice in it?

When we attempt to live the Gospel amid the complexities of contemporary society, we hit against plenty of problems. Making decisions about what to say or do as a disciple of Jesus Christ is not often straightforward. Frequently we are driven to compromises which seem far removed from the forthrightness of the Lord.

The business and commercial worlds with their competitions and power struggles, the educational and medical worlds with their hierarchies and traditions, the government and civil service worlds with their responsibilities and rules, the social welfare and trade-union worlds with their policies and confrontations – it is difficult to discern whether gaining a market, putting through a reform, increasing overall efficiency, or turning a blind eye to minor infringements of the system, uphold or deny Christian principles.

Strikes highlight the difficulty. Christians are nearly always against strikes, especially those that seem to injure the innocent and the helpless. A strike among hospital staff brings a barrage of denunciation from Church leaders. Yet sometimes the causes of such strikes are high-handedness and mismanagement of a kind that Christians should also be protesting about.

Most English Christians shy away from what appear to be overt political demonstrations. We prefer to give the powers that be the benefit of the doubt when questions are raised about maladministration or injustices. We should like, in the words of the second collect at Evening Prayer, 'to pass our time in rest and quietness'.

But rest and quietness are only established, as the collect reminds us, as long as we are 'being freed from the fear of our enemies'. And in our society today there are plenty of enemies within the gates whom we have to oppose.

Take racism, for example. With anti-semitism it is the most destructive force we have to combat. Acts of Parliament against discrimination give some protection, but laws do not change deep-seated attitudes. Fear of other ethnic groups persists even in Christian congregations. Black people have been shown they are unwelcome in some churches.

Yet elsewhere Christians have been in the forefront of the battle. In a town where a man born in India was being threatened by an order for an unjust deportation, a group of Christians undertook a three-day 'sanctuary fast' in one of the local churches to pray for him. From another town three Christians visited Bangladesh to trace people who had been refused permission to join their families in this country and proved the continued separation was contrary to British law.

These were little more than gestures, but their impact was wide. Not least important was the growing realisation among men and women of other faiths in those towns that some followers of Jesus Christ were prepared to make sacrifices to preserve the unity of family life which their Gospel proclaimed.

In struggles against racism and other forms of social injustice, we find ourselves among unexpected allies.

I once had to organise a march by the Christian churches in Manchester against the National Front. It was astonishing how quickly the project was supported by all kinds of political and community groups, trades unions and other organisations. As I looked back at the 2,000-strong march, I could see a few trade-union banners and political slogans among the processional crosses and church banners which the clergy and people had brought with them for the demonstration. It was a curious mixture. No doubt some joined our march to promote their own ends. But many were impressed at the strength of the churches' support. And I had the strong feeling that for once I was with Jesus Christ in the highways and byways of our society instead of just within ecclesiastical gatherings.

Similarly when we stand for distinctly religious values, we find ourselves attracting people of other faiths to our cause. In Britain today about 800,000 adherents of other faiths worship regularly each week compared with about 1.8 million Anglicans and 1.5 million Roman Catholics. There are more Muslims in this country than Methodists.

One way of getting to know members of those religious groups is to show concern for their welfare. The dialogue with them then begins with mutual respect. The break-up of the family, unemployment among the young, the lack of moral standards in what is presented as entertainment – it is not only Christians who protest about these things. The sincere Jew, Muslim, Sikh, Buddhist and Hindu all react against many of these evils in the same way.

A few days before the visit of Pope John Paul II to Manchester, it was my task to visit an imam who was to be presented to his Holiness. Because of the Falklands campaign, we did not know whether the Pope would come to Britain or not. The imam listened as I explained the security precautions surrounding the Pope's visit (which entailed, among other things, the imam having his photograph and fingerprints taken!), and then the conversation moved on to the uncertainty of the event.

When he took me to the door, the imam looked at me gravely and said, 'We are praying that the Pope can come!'

Britain is one of the most multiracial countries in the

world – in varieties of ethnic groupings if not in proportion to numbers. It is also a land which contains adherents of the world's major religions. We have an opportunity of demonstrating how the different peoples and faiths of our global village can live together as a model for the rest of the world.

Perhaps one of the greatest exports from these islands in the past has been the tolerance and mutual respect which made it possible for a democratic government to be established. Could racial tolerance and mutual respect for different ethnic groups be the next great export?

It could, if Christians were at the heart of the struggle for racial equality with their Gospel of forgiveness and reconciliation.

'What can we do to hasten the time, the time that shall surely be,
When the earth shall be filled with the glory of God as the waters cover the sea?'

A.C. Ainger's hymn was written in the heyday of missionary enterprise at the end of the nineteenth century, with its vision of the whole world responding to the Gospel of the kingdom. That enterprise has changed its character since then. An awareness of partnership has replaced the patronage of the older Churches of the West, and white Christians are having to get used to the statistical fact that they are almost outnumbered by black Christians in the population of this planet.

Christians are world citizens as well as British, American, Australian, New Zealanders, Canadians, and so on, and there is emerging a world Christian conscience of which each of us is a part. It is no longer possible to discuss issues narrowly from a British viewpoint. The debate on 'The Church and the Bomb' in the General Synod of the Church of England, for example, took place amid signs of a growing movement among Christians in the western world for unilateral nuclear disarmament.

In recent years the Churches in the Pacific have reported on the appalling effects of the sixty-six nuclear bombs tested under strictly controlled conditions on the Marshall Islands. Although it is now nearly a quarter of a century since the last bomb was tested there, babies are still being born like lumps of shapeless, transparent jelly, foetuses have been delivered out of their mothers' mouths, and children have come into the world with six fingers on each hand and with orifices in the wrong parts of their bodies.

TV programmes have been produced (and some of them suppressed) depicting the effects of a nuclear war on countries like Britain and the USA. The Society of Friends has pioneered a scheme to record its conscious objection to the payment of taxes for money spent on nuclear armaments. That could very well develop into something much more widespread in the years to come.

Christians in western countries are moving together, too, in favour of proposals for a more just share out of the world's resources. The Brandt Commission's report was a catalyst that stimulated prayer and discussion on what it means to live in a world created by God and inhabited by those who look forward to the signs of his justice and peace.

Meetings with Christians from Third World countries put the debate about the nuclear bomb in another perspective. A bishop from India remarked that the people of the villages he knew were more concerned about survival now rather than about a future holocaust.

'You in the West are worried about what might happen to your children in years to come,' he said; 'my people are worried that their children might starve tomorrow.'

With a world view comes a Christian contribution to the campaign for human rights. Amnesty International and other agencies work patiently to expose injustices – executions, torture, deprivation of freedom, slavery, and other forms of inhumanity.

The modern communications miracle makes it all the

more obvious that we need to learn to live and share together. Within a few years it will be possible to receive on our TV sets programmes transmitted by satellite from anywhere in the world. The opportunities for gathering information and for sending it out will be enormous. Since the Gospel is essentially about communication, Christians have a vital interest in this, too.

How can we respond to this bewilderingly complicated and vast problem?

Be selective. Specialise in one or two matters for concern in the world. Do your homework: get to know about it. Find out if other Christians have the same concern. One of my jobs as an ecumenical officer is to put Christian groups with similar interests in touch with one another and with the numerous agencies which can supply information and educational material.

Then wait for the Lord to provide you with an opportunity for using your material in letters of protest to the newspapers and Members of Parliament and in meetings to rouse local interest. The modern media makes it possible for pressure groups to be heard nationwide. Make use of it.

A small group in a Roman Catholic parish, encouraged by their denomination's Commission for Justice and Peace, made a study of the Philippines. They wrote to the head-quarters of two or three multinational companies with interests in the islands, familiarising themselves with those companies' involvement and making enquiries about the working conditions of their employees there. Documents from the World Council of Churches and other bodies filled out their files.

Eventually, items of news prompted them to investigate further, and they discovered that one of the companies was suspected of being sympathetic towards the operations of a certain death squad which was murdering the owners of smallholdings who were holding up some expansion by one of the companies' agents. The Roman Catholic group sent the information to a Member of Parliament, and his questions to the British government caused a loan to that company to be suspended until further enquiries were made.

I should emphasise that none of the group was a specialist in multinational companies or international affairs. They were simply ordinary Roman Catholics who undertook the Justice and Peace project out of interest – and then were able to use that interest for the benefit of some Filipinos on the other side of the world.

In the Templeton address which he gave in the Guildhall, London, in 1983, Alexander Solzhenitsyn said that it was the weakness of Christian witness in Russia at the beginning of this century which made the Russian revolution possible. He said:

> The events of the Russian revolution can only be understood now, at the end of the century, against the background of what has since occurred in the rest of the world. What emerges here is a process of universal significance. And if I were called upon to identify briefly the principal trait of the entire twentieth century, here too, I would be unable to find anything more precise and pithy than to say, 'Men had forgotten God.'[3]

It is tempting to let Solzhenitsyn have the last word in this chapter. But I must add one other to adjust the balance.

It is this. As disciples of Jesus Christ, we must not allow ourselves to become so absorbed with the affairs of this world that we forget we are destined for a city which is to come. We may be world citizens in one sense, but in another sense we are merely sojourners – tourists through a foreign country. This present life with its joys and pains is temporal; the life God offers us in Christ is eternal.

Belief in eternal life is not a kind of appendix to the Gospel. It is the motive for living now. Because Jesus rose from the dead, the foretaste of eternal life is brought to us now and intimately related to how we spend our time here.

It does not make us less caring about the circumstances under which people live and work in this world, but it puts our caring in the kingdom-goal perspective which is so necessary if we are to follow Jesus and not some man-dreamt-up fantasy of him.

'Set your minds on things that are above, not on things that are on earth. For you have died, and your life is hid with Christ in God' (Col. 3: 2–4).

[1] Jim Wallis, *The Call to Conversion* (Lion, 1981), p. 9.
[2] Ibid, p. 129.
[3] *The Times*, May 11th, 1983.

CHAPTER 9

The Devil's Blasts

Sometime during the thirteenth century, a group of English nuns asked their spiritual director why it was that Christians seemed to be subject to greater temptations the more they tried to serve God.

He replied: 'Let no one of holy life think she will not be tempted. The good, who have climbed high, are more greatly tempted than the weak. And this is to be expected, for the higher the hill the more the wind blows. The higher the hill of holy, exalted life, the more and the stronger will be the devil's blasts and the winds of temptation.'[1]

One way and another, those nuns' experience is common to all Christians. For weeks, perhaps longer, our lives are peaceful. We are conscious of some failings, but they don't seem very serious. We ask the Lord to forgive us and take them away. Then, as unexpectedly as a summer storm, temptations gust in. In the squalls we heel over and plunge into sin.

We're ashamed. How could that have happened to us when God was being so good to us?

I've noticed these attacks often assail me just before or just after some ministry in which God's grace has been evident. When I'm preparing to lead a service in church, or after I've returned from speaking at a weekend conference, then I'm most vulnerable. What does God think he's doing? I ask myself indignantly – and then remember James 1: 13, 'Let no one say when he is tempted, "I am tempted by God"; for God cannot be tempted with evil and he himself tempts no one.'

No, temptations come from elsewhere. Their human origins are complex. Deep inside us are destructive and rebellious impulses seeking outlets. Early experiences of babyhood and childhood leave their digits on the computer-reflexes which influence our attitudes and desires later in life. Give a child everything he or she expects in the first years of life, and that child will grow up with undisciplined selfishness and greed dominant in his or her character.

Then there is the mysterious transmission of genetic traits and the effect of physical, mental and emotional strains on us now. These also influence thoughts and feelings, desires and reactions. So do severe injuries, medical treatment and burdensome responsibilities. Add to these the pressures of personal relationships and environment, plus the mysterious effect of collective evil and the spiritual forces behind it, and we have the sum total of destructiveness which the Church has long categorised as 'the world, the flesh, and the devil'.

1. *The World*, in this context, stands for humanity in its corporate opposition to God. Although created by God, men and women are permeated with evil, an infestation none of us can avoid. Theologians call it original sin. The theme runs through the New Testament but appears most clearly in the fourth gospel, where the world is pronounced to be ignorant of God (John 1: 10, 11, 18), to hate Christ because its works are evil (7: 7), and to reject the followers of Jesus (15: 19; 17: 14). Although the disciples are in the world, they are not of the world (17: 16).

The influence of the world on us is not easy to discern. We are products of our age and our society. We imbile assumptions and values from those around us from the moment we are born.

When we look at what we call Christian living more closely, it often turns out to be nothing more than western, middle-class culture. Most of us would regard a decent job, a mortgage-free house, a prudent investment in a building society, and a good school for our children as 'Christian' objectives. But are they?

In my experience as a clergyman, I have been startled to find the world pushing its influence into all kinds of areas of Church life. When I resigned as a parish priest to join the community at Whatcombe, one or two friends more or less implied I was committing professional suicide! 'Won't it ruin your career prospects in the Church?' one of them asked.

'Don't let the world squeeze you into its own mould,' is J.B. Phillips's inspired translation of Romans 12: 2.

2. *The Flesh*. In Christian moral theology the desires of the flesh are known as concupiscence, from the Latin, *concupisco*, 'to desire eagerly'.

Desires in themselves, of course, are not necessarily evil. The impulse to survive and to procreate are necessary for the continuation of the human race. Desires to be fulfilled in life are not wrong provided they are free of selfishness and subservient to God's will. It is when they dislodge God's purposes for us that they become sinful.

Behind concupiscence is the deeper sin of pride. We claim to be disciples of Jesus Christ, but inwardly we keep decisions in our hands. Instead of being dependent on him, we try to assert our independence. We know that God has a plan for us. We know that our greater happiness and welfare lie with him. Yet we still rebel.

Dying to ourselves has much to do with rejecting the influence of pride in our lives. When Jesus said, 'If any man would come after me, let him deny himself and take up his cross and follow me' (Mark 8: 34), the word 'deny' meant turning one's back on personal desires. The same word is used in Mark 14: 68 where Peter disclaimed any connection with the prisoner, Jesus. It is a condition of discipleship that we disclaim every link that ties us to humanity in its pride, selfishness, ambition – all the things which reject the sovereignty of God.

As we have seen, Paul contrasted living in the flesh with living by the Spirit. Dying to self and rising to Christ can only be effected by our repentance and our willingness to receive the Spirit. Yet pride can make us unwilling to accept that liberation. That is what makes it the deadliest of sins. It was the sin of Eden. 'You will be like gods,' said the serpent (Gen. 3: 5, TEV margin): the highest temptation is to want to put ourselves on a level with God so that we can claim for ourselves mastery of our destiny, seeking to do for ourselves what can only be done by him.

3. *The Devil.* The ultimate source of evil is in that objective, powerful, cunning and deadly force known in the Bible under various names. I'm not concerned here to get involved in an argument on what we mean by 'a personal devil'. My concern is that we recognise evil as the enemy behind all spiritual enemies – in ourselves, in others, in human groups, in the structures that make up our society, and in the ebb and flow of national and international affairs.

To renounce Satan is not to reject some mythological being in whose existence some do not believe. It is to reject the entire world of darkness and deceit, lies and hatred, pain and injustice, which cruelly destroy human beings and their relationships.

Deceit is one of his most dangerous weapons. He deceives us about the ideas and values we have as Christians. He falsifies and counterfeits the truth the Church is commissioned to proclaim. He causes us to mistake white for black and black for white. He disrupts the fellowship of the body of Christ by stirring up strife where there should be love. He trails in the wake of the Holy Spirit's work, scheming to destroy what is good.

The prescription in 1 Peter for defeating the devil is humility and watchfulness. Humility does not mean a negative kind of self-abandonment; it means a deliberate attitude of total trust in God, knowing that he is the one who has conquered the enemy: 'Humble yourselves therefore under the mighty hand of God, that in due time he may exalt you. Cast all your anxieties on him, for he cares about you' (5: 6–7). Watchfulness ensures that we are not lulled into a false sense of security: 'Be sober, be watchful . . . Resist him,

firm in your faith' (5: 8–9) – not 'the faith', that is, the belief
of Christians, but positive faith, trust in God.

In the early Church the candidate for baptism was made
to spit upon the devil as part of the ritual. We may not want
to restore the custom to our revised baptismal liturgies, but
the challenge is the same! War is declared on the devil when
we become disciples of Jesus Christ, and we can be sure
Satan will spit back at us.

So we should not expose ourselves to practices associated
with evil influences – from horoscopes and ouija to
spiritualism and witchcraft. Video nasties are a modern
danger area, too.

In our own lives we need wisdom to discern between what
stems from the devil and what comes from the influence of
the world and the flesh. There is an unhealthy tendency in
some quarters to attribute everything to the devil, thus
diverting us from the need for deeper penitence and more
self-discipline. It is not usually the direct action of the devil
that causes us to get up feeling out of sorts, to get angry with
the children and to have a row with a friend. Those things
usually mean that we need to come to the cross of Christ, to
crucify the flesh with its passions and desires, and to receive
more of the love of God into our lives through the Holy
Spirit.

Yet there are occasions when it is not just the influence of
the world and the flesh which crushes us. Then we need once
again privately to renounce the devil once more and perhaps
to ask others to pray for our deliverance from evil (in more
serious cases under the pastoral leadership of the local
church).

One night, after visiting my wife, Margaret, in hospital,
where a doctor with a grave face had told me she was
dangerously ill, I drove away in the dark and rain with an
inner emptiness that I had never known before. The thud of
the car's windscreen wipers sounded like the drum of doom.
Tears flooded my eyes. I stopped the car and slumped in the
seat. I felt as if an intolerable burden was crushing me

through the floor of the vehicle into the ground.

Then, deliberately, I braced myself to ask for deliverance from this evil oppression. I do not remember exactly what I said, but it was something like this:

'Spirit of despair, get away from me! In the name of Jesus Christ, I renounce you! Go! Go! Go to the place prepared for you by God! Father in heaven, I ask you to release me through the blood of your Son, my Saviour and my Lord!'

I prayed for a few moments in tongues, turning my thoughts to the Holy Spirit and his infilling power.

Quite swiftly, the feeling of emptiness and the sense of burden were lifted from me. It was like seeing the curtains go up in a darkened theatre and a glorious scene in bright lights come into view. There spread over me an assurance of God's love for Margaret and for me, and I knew that we were in his hands.

I started the engine and drove off, singing a chorus. I had to go that night to give a lecture to some black pastors from Afro-Caribbean congregations in Manchester. I told them of Margaret's illness and asked them to pray for her. This they did, with resounding fervour.

Afterwards one of them came up to me and squeezed my hand.

'De good Lord ha' tol' me your missus's gonna be well again!' he said.

Praise God, it was an authentic prophecy! She did get well.

If we are to be on our guard against the temptations of the world, the flesh and the devil, we need to know something of the nature of temptation itself.

In some modern versions of the Bible the word temptation is translated 'testing'. That sets the experience in God's perspective. He allows us to be tempted so that our discipleship may be tested and consequently strengthened.

It is a condition of our human existence that, being given the freedom to choose to respond to his call, that choice can be assailed at any time. We are still in this world in that interim period between the mortal blow dealt to Satan on the cross and the final destruction of his dark kingdom when the Lord comes again. Temptations are the signs of the spiritual warfare.

In Jesus, God took human nature and met face to face the full force of the devil's power and conquered it as man in the power of the Spirit. That same indwelling presence of God is available to us as well. Hence Paul could assure his troubled congregation, 'God is faithful and he will not let you be tempted beyond your strength, but with the temptation will also provide the way of escape, that you may be able to endure it' (1 Cor. 10: 13). A successful battle against temptations can become one of those seasons of grace in which we grow in spiritual maturity.

Discerning the approach of a temptation is the task of our conscience. This is the name we give to the process whereby we hear God's voice within us and allow him to affect our reasoning mechanism. The biblical term for conscience is the heart, in which God's will is written (Rom. 2: 15). Our consciences need to be educated so that the mind of Christ can be formed in us. Openness to the Holy Spirit and commitment to the Church, with all that this involves as sketched in this book, are the means of receiving this formation.

This does not mean that we become infallible. Making mistakes can be a part of educating our consciences. And if we make mistakes because we have rejected what God has been telling us through these means, then we are blameworthy. Christians who are certain they know the mind of Christ because they've studied the Bible make mistakes because they have refused to listen to God's voice through others – other Christians of different traditions and sometimes those other people who, although they are non-Christians, are nevertheless used by God to reveal aspects of his will which have been hidden from us. Here again, humility is an important prerequisite.

When we are tempted, then, an alarm-bell rings in our consciences. Francis de Sales (1567–1622), the saintly Bishop of Geneva during the difficult post-Reformation period, had some helpful advice to give on this. In his book, *Introduction to the Devout Life,* he distinguished three stages in the approach of temptations.

The first stage he called 'the suggestion'. Prompted by our desires or our imaginations, a temptation presents itself to us before we have a chance to react to it. I see an apple belonging to someone else on a table. There is no one about. Suddenly I realise I could take the apple without anyone seeing me. Maybe they wouldn't even notice the apple was missing. That is the 'suggestion' stage.

The next stage he called 'the delight'. That is when the suggestion becomes attractive to us. We feel the pull of it. My mind dwells on the rosy colour of the apple and imagines how juicy and sweet it would be to eat. It is at this stage that our conscience is awakened and a struggle begins within us.

'This is that warfare which the apostle describes when he says that "the flesh lusteth against the spirit,"' wrote de Sales.[2] Clearly, this is the moment to say, No!

De Sales also pointed out that neither of these first two stages is sinful in itself. My mouth may water at the sight of the apple, but while I'm rejecting the temptation I'm still on God's side. His grace is working through me in the struggle.

'As long as we remain steadfast in our resolution to take no pleasure in the temptation,' said the bishop, 'it is utterly impossible that we should offend God.[3]

It is when we slip into the third stage, which he called 'the consent', that we become sinners. I can no longer resist the apple. I know it is wrong – my conscience tells me so – but I stretch out a hand and take it, determined to eat it as soon as I can. (Of course, if at that moment I suddenly become so guilty that I return the apple, you could say I have reversed the effect of 'the consent'. But it was a brush with evil, and it might be right for me to admit to the owner of the apple what I tried to do!)

Jesus is our example in refuting temptations. After his experience of being baptised in the Jordan and of fasting in the desert, the devil put suggestions to him that would have caused Jesus to reject his Father's will. The devil even quoted scripture in presenting the temptations.

But Jesus did not allow the temptations to get beyond what de Sales called the first stage. He countered them by quoting scripture as well: '"You shall worship the Lord your God and him only shall you serve"' – '"Man shall not live by bread alone"' – '"You shall not tempt the Lord your God"' (Luke 4: 8, 4 and 12). What is significant about the passages he quoted from the law of Moses (Deut. 6: 16; 8: 3 and 6: 13) is that they laid down the principles on which the chosen people were to occupy the promised land. These quotations reveal that the second Joshua (= 'God is salvation') was leading the new Israel into the promised land of God's kingdom and his disciples were to follow him, provided they also accepted the principles of obedience which Jesus' life and teaching enshrined. In other words, they had to fight against temptations, too.

It is easier to reject a temptation at the first stage. But that is not always possible in certain situations, and so we find ourselves involved in spiritual combat. We invoke the Holy Spirit; we put on the whole armour of God (Eph. 6: 14–17). There are all kinds of stratagems: arrow prayers, speaking in tongues, recalling passages of scripture which promise the Lord's aid, switching our minds on to something else, seeking the support of other Christians' prayers.

And we can counter-attack. The sword of the Spirit is a weapon of attack as well as defence. We counter-attack by asking God to give us the virtue or fruit of the Spirit which is the opposite of the sin which the temptation suggests.

In Galatians 5: 19–24 Paul sets out sins and virtues in opposite ranks, like the soldiers of opposing armies drawn up ready for battle.

On one side he put fornication, impurity, licentiousness, idolatry, sorcery, enmity, strife, jealousy, anger, selfishness, dissension, party spirit, envy, drunkenness and carousing. (Perhaps this list was based on a moral code used for catechetical purposes in the instruction of converts in the apostolic Church.)

On the other side he set the fruit of the Spirit: love, joy, peace, patience, kindness, goodness, faithfulness, gentleness, self-control. Together they sum up the personality of Jesus Christ as he is presented to us in the Gospels. In the power of God, said the apostle, these virtues were unconquerable.

But soldiers should train beforehand if they are to be effective in battle. This is true of us. We shouldn't wait until we're tempted before we arm ourselves to fight against a persistent temptation. We should ask for it and practise it in daily life. If we are tempted to meanness, we should pray for and watch out for opportunities for the virtue of generosity; or if we are tempted to sudden anger, we should seek to be more patient.

De Sales counselled this: 'In time of peace, that is, when temptations to the sin to which you are most inclined do not molest you, make several acts of contrary virtue. If occasions to do so do not present themselves, endeavour to seek them out. By this means you will strengthen your heart against future temptations.'[4]

Some of us are more susceptible to temptations than others. As we have different gifts, so we have different weaknesses! This is where laws about right and wrong have to be understood in the light of a loving concern for the person involved. Jesus accepted the law of Moses, but he recognised that it had its limitations. He healed on the sabbath when the needs of an individual required it, even though he was breaking the law in the eyes of the interpreters of it in his day.

What is known as casuistry – that is to say, the art of discerning what is right or wrong for a particular individual in circumstances where the general norms are not precise enough – goes back to the Greek philosophers. Unfortunately casuistry has got a bad name for it has been used in the past as a device for excusing misdemeanours and avoiding responsibilities. But in essence it is the business of ensuring that the letter of the law serves the purposes of the Holy Spirit and not the opposite. The advice of other, mature Christians is usually needed if we are to avoid self-deception or over-scrupulosity in decisions about moral problems in our own lives.

But, alas, victory over temptation is not always ours. We are still liable to surrender to the world, the flesh and the devil, and to fall into sin. What then?

The steps we should take are set out in the form of general confession used in many church services. As we examine it, we shall see that it is, line by line, a kind of spiritual step-ladder showing us how to receive the forgiveness of God and to be received by him as a son or daughter through adoption in Jesus Christ. This old formulary has within it the wisdom of centuries of devout reflection on scriptural teaching.

Almighty God, our heavenly Father

God is a loving Father as well as a merciful judge. Through our union with Jesus Christ we are able 'with confidence [to] draw near to the throne of grace, that we may receive mercy and find grace to help in time of need' (Heb. 4: 16). The mediatorial role of Jesus is recalled later in the prayer.

It is understood, of course, that we can only ask forgiveness of God if we have forgiven those who have wronged us: 'Forgive us our sins as we forgive those who sin against us.' God can only forgive and use in his ministry of reconciliation those who, by their own forgiveness of others, are his peacemakers. This is underlined in the parable of the unforgiving servant (Luke 16: 1–13) and in the example of Jesus himself, who prayed for the forgiveness of his executioners, an example followed by Stephen (Acts 7: 60).

We have sinned against you and against our fellow men

Every sin we commit, no matter how private, is an offence against other members of the Church. In his teaching on the unity of the Christian community, with members exercising spiritual gifts for their mutual upbuilding, Paul pointed out that sins have the directly opposite effects to gifts: they weaken the whole body. 'If one member suffers, all suffer together' (1 Cor. 12: 26). The analogy of the Church with a physical body is illuminating here: if one part of our body is unhealthy, other parts are affected as well and they cannot function properly.

New Testament congregations had a procedure for dealing with the serious, unrepentant offender in their midst. They separated him or her from their fellowship until he or she asked for prayer for forgiveness.

Paul likened the presence of the sinner in the congregation to the presence of leaven in the Jewish house at Passover time. In this case leaven was regarded as ritually unclean, and the Jewish mother had the duty of searching her home to make sure that no leaven was left anywhere before the Passover celebrations began. The new unleavened bread of the feast symbolised a new beginning, not to be contaminated by leaven from older bakings. Similarly, Christians were not to be contaminated by mixing with sinners who had not turned their backs on the world, the flesh and the devil: 'Cleanse out the old leaven that you may be a new lump, as you really are unleavened' (1 Cor. 5: 7).

The discipline of excommunication has fallen into disuse, but the scriptural truth that it represented remains. Asking for God's forgiveness is properly done within the Christian fellowship, and this is why acts of general confession are included in church services. But if we feel our sin is a grievous one, then it is wise to make a confession of it in the presence of a priest or minister. He or she is then able to pray for our forgiveness and pronounce the absolution of our sins with the authority of Jesus Christ in his Church.

We may be asked to abstain from Communion if an

amendment of our lives has to be made. For example, if we confess that we have had a row with someone and not apologised, we should offer that apology before we share in the eucharist again.

Saying sorry is never easy, yet it can be the beginnings of a new relationship. It can also have a kaleidoscope effect. When two who have quarrelled are seen to forgive one another, it becomes a spiritual gift to the congregation, encouraging them to exercise forgiveness in their lives, too. The quarrel between Paul and Barnabas over John Mark was apparently buried later (I Cor. 9: 6 and Acts 15: 36–41), but at least it had the effect of initiating two missionary enterprises instead of one – Barnabas to Cyprus and Paul to Syria and Cilicia.

But what if the other refuses to be reconciled with us? That is a matter between that person and the Lord. We've said we're sorry; we've offered to try and put right anything that is wrong in the relationship. We can do no more. Perhaps the other has some deeper psychological reason for wanting to feel aggrieved with us. Many people nurse all kinds of emotional hurts and physical weaknesses as a perverse form of self-expression. They need our prayers for healing.

in thought and word and deed

These are the basic human faculties through which our disobedience is manifested – the rebellious and angry thoughts we harbour against God and against others, the lying and unloving words we use, and the things we do alone and with others. When we make an act of self-examination, we should see if the sins we have remembered are attached to further, less obvious offences. Did the lie we told spring from a hidden fear? Did the slap we gave a child in anger stem from an undetected resentment? Sins are rarely solitary; one offence is usually accompanied by a small cluster of companions which also require the forgiveness of God.

in the evil we have done
and the good we have not done

These are what moralists call the sins of commission and the sins of omission. We tend to feel less guilty about the sins of omission, although not to do what God has commanded is just as disobedient as doing what he has forbidden.

through ignorance, through weakness,
through our own deliberate fault

There are sins which are unintentional. We may not be blamed for them, except in so far as we have neglected opportunities to learn about them, but nevertheless they are acts of disobedience against God.

There are sins which result from some personal weakness which has not yet been strengthened by the Holy Spirit. They are not grievous sins, in that the damage they do to our relationships with God and with one another is small. As soon as we realise what we have done, we immediately make an act of contrition and seek God's forgiveness. These sins are known as venial, dishabilitating but not deadly in the life of the Christian and of the Church.

And then there are sins which are deliberate and intentional. We choose to do what we know is against God's will, even though our conscience is ringing alarm-bells. It is the kind of choice that Adam and Eve made and its effect is to kill the relationship between God and ourselves: hence its title, mortal sin.

There is a rough-and-ready character about the threefold distinction. Often we are not entirely blameless because we are ignorant of certain sins, and venial sins can become mortal if they persist. But the classification has some value in helping us to achieve a balanced view of our failings – avoiding excessive scrupulosity and morbidity on one hand and insensitive carelessness and superficiality on the other.

We are truly sorry and repent of all our sins

`he phrase brings together the more familiar word 'sorry'
vith the biblical word 'repent'. We associate the former with
eelings, although we may not always feel sorry for a sin,
specially if our appreciation of the effects of disobedience
o God is limited. To be sorry, therefore, is more than to
ave a feeling of regret; it is an awareness that we have
separated ourselves from the love of God and aligned
ourselves with the evil which brought his Son Jesus Christ to
he cross.

To repent is to turn round, to be reconverted, towards
Christ. It is a desire to resume our pilgrimage as his disciple,
a pilgrimage we undertook when we first repented and were
baptised. Like the prodigal, we have come to ourselves and
decided to return to the Father.

For the sake of your Son, Jesus Christ,
who died for us,
forgive us all that is past

The appeal to God the Father, as we have just seen, is made
through his Son, who is our mediator in heaven and who
'offered for all time a single sacrifice for sins' (Heb. 10: 12).
The atoning and redeeming work of God becomes relevant
to us in a profoundly personal way at the moment when we
ask for forgiveness. Now the cross has a meaning which is
deeper than it usually has when we hear sermons about the
sacrifice of Calvary or when we sing hymns about it. Unless
we are humbling ourselves in body, mind and spirit at the
foot of the cross, God cannot receive us back as his sons and
daughters.

But, again, we don't earn our forgiveness by the genuine-
ness of our sorrow and repentance. It is the desire to be
accepted as a disciple of Christ and to walk with him by the
power of the Spirit that matters on our side. That desire may

be feeble or confused, but it is the direction in which we want to go in our hearts that counts. God knows better than ourselves what we really want.

> *And grant that we may serve you*
> *in newness of life*
> *to the glory of your Name*

What indicates the direction in which we want to go is the resolve not to sin again and the act of fresh commitment through the renewing power of the Holy Spirit. Changes in our lives spring from such moments. As we saw in the letters quoted in the second chapter of this book, it was out of a realisation of their need for forgiveness that the two writers moved to a position of openness to God and received a new infilling of the Holy Spirit. The experience of falling into sin and of being forgiven by God (and sometimes by others) motivates us to seek his grace further. Out of our weakness we can in this way win God's strength.

'Rabbi, who sinned, this man or his parents, that he was born blind?' the disciples asked Jesus one day.

The suspicion still persists in some quarters that ill-health is one of the ways God punishes the sinner.

To dismiss this suspicion is not to say there is *never* a connection between our sins and our sickness. Obviously if we overeat or neglect to take exercise, ill-health can result from our self-indulgence and sloth. But that is far removed from the Christian belief that ill-health and death as they affect mankind are signs of mankind's rejection of God.

Furthermore, the biblical understanding of the salvation God offers us through his Son is wholeness or healthfulness in the fullest sense – wholeness of body and mind as well as of spirit. Hence the ministry of healing is linked with the ministry of reconciliation – a foretaste of the kingdom of God.

Whether that healing comes through the skill of medical care, or the ministry of those gifted by the Holy Spirit, or (as is more usual) a combination of both, then we should prepare for it by confessing our sins in one of the ways suggested above. Before he healed the paralysed man, Jesus pronounced that the sick man's sins has been forgiven (Mark 2: 1–10), and confession and the anointing of the sick are brought together in the epistle of James (5: 14–16).

In practical terms, it means this: we should pray for healing when we are ill, examining our consciences as we do so. But if the illness is serious enough to require medical treatment and perhaps a spell in hospital, then we'd be wise to make our confession to a priest or a minister and to receive anointing with the laying-on of hands at home, in a prayer-group, or in a service of prayer for healing.

Assured of God's forgiveness through the cross of Jesus Christ, we can commit ourselves confidently into his care, expecting him to show his love for us in whatever happens.

Usually we are healed, suddenly or gradually. That can be a step of faith in our pilgrimage and a cause of thanksgiving to God. But what if physical healing does not come? What if the illness persists and gets worse?

I have no wish to try and minimise the depressing and dehumanising effects of a long illness or a permanent disability. The nagging persistence of pain, the humiliation of dependence on others, the frustrations arising from our thoughts and feelings, the sense of despair as one week follows another – all these can add up to a crushing burden.

Yet it is precisely in such cases that God can transfigure his children.

While this book was being written, I visited a Christian lady who was dying of cancer – she died, in fact, just about the time the first draft was completed.

She had difficult moments when she depended much on Christian friends and on the skill of the staff of the hospice where she was taken in her final weeks. I've known her for years, but I was quite unprepared to witness in her the rapid

undergirding of the peace of God in the midst of her
sufferings.

She looked forward to dying. It was easier to talk about
death with her than with anyone else I've ever met. She
praised God because she was drawing near to the climax of
the redemption Jesus Christ had won for her on the cross.
For her, death was her healing, her salvation. Before drugs
clouded her consciousness, I sensed more and more that it
was no longer my friend who lived but Christ who lived in
her.

The privilege of witnessing her passover taught me yet
again that, if we live by the Spirit, then we are drawn into
that mysterious communion with the sufferings of Christ
which are a prelude to our resurrection and eternal life with
him.

It is a mystery we can expound from the scriptures but
never explain. It is a mystery we can illustrate from the
stories of the saints but never teach. It is a mystery we can
witness in others and hope to experience when suffering and
death come to us.

It does nothing for those who ask, even sincerely, 'Why
does God allow such suffering to happen?'

John Richards has written a prayer, based on 2 Corinthians 12: 7-10, which expresses this mystery beautifully:

Heavenly Father,
whose Son Jesus Christ
    was wounded for our transgressions
    and bruised for our iniquities:

[1] Gerald Sitwell (ed.), *The Ancrene Riwle* (Burns and Oates, 1963), p. 78.
[2] Francis de Sales, *Introduction to the Devout Life*, edited by John K.
Ryan (Longmans, 1956), p. 264.
[3] Ibid, p. 263.
[4] Ibid, p. 278.
[5] In *Twenty-four Healing Prayers* (Renewal Servicing, P.O. Box 366,
Addlestone, Weybridge, Surrey KT15 3UL).

come to us in our sufferings,
and hold us in your all-sufficient grace,
that your power may be made perfect in our weakness;
   in the name of him who died and rose again for us,
   Jesus Christ our Lord.[5]

CHAPTER 10

Giving Thanks

The theme of this book is that to live by the Spirit is to encounter God at every turn.

At home and at work, in the local church and in the neighbourhood, the Holy Spirit strengthens us to discern and to share in God's mission in his world. And we have noted, like the roads on the route-planning map I mentioned in the introduction, the kind of guidance and equipping we might expect from God in various situations.

It remains for us in this last chapter to focus on the place where our discipleship finds its inspiration and renewal – in the worship of the Church.

Through worship God cleanses us, forgives us, speaks to us, feeds us and encourages us. That is why worship is central to discipleship. 'It is our duty at all times and in all places' to give God thanks and praise. What I propose to do is to take the liturgy of the eucharist in its traditional form and show how it becomes the means of spiritual renewal in those aspects of discipleship we have discussed. I shall not refer back to points made in previous chapters. I hope the relevance of what I say will be obvious without that.

To celebrate the eucharist we have to gather with other Christians – with the members of our own household, at least. We can't celebrate the eucharist by ourselves. Prayer can be an individual activity, but eucharistic worship has to be done corporately, even if only with two or three.

Coming together with others is in itself a sign of commitment. We join with others in God's family. We make a response to Christ's call to gather in his name. We show we're available to him and to his Church. Whatever our private arrangements, we set them on one side in order to assemble.

'Let us consider how to stir up one another to love and good works, not neglecting to meet together, as is the habit of some, but encouraging one another, and all the more as you see the Day drawing near' (Heb. 10: 24-5). To cease to worship is to begin to cut oneself off from the life-line of our pilgrimage.

We greet one another in the giving of the peace. Disciples cannot act as if they were individuals. In Christ we are one with another, bound to one another in the fellowship of the Spirit.

No doubt there are limitations in our mutual commitment. A black woman in a church noted how a white woman, who usually sat in the pew in front, quickly put her gloves on before she turned to shake the black woman's hand in the giving of the peace at the parish Communion. We may put on all kinds of mental and psychological gloves when we reach out to others, but the liturgy still gently urges us to stretch out our hands knowing that one day the gloves will have to come off.

At some point in the service we are required to make a corporate act of confession. We are challenged to die yet again to those moods, thoughts and actions that separate us from God and from others. The pronouncing of the absolution and the giving of the peace are intimately associated with one another. To be Christ's disciples we need to be reconciled to one another as well as to God.

Absolution and peace, then, are the doors of worship. To refuse reconciliation is to stay outside those doors, no matter how heartily we join in the hymns or how often we go up to the communion rail to receive the sacrament.

Jesus told the Samaritan woman that the time was coming – indeed, it had already come – when 'true worshippers will worship the Father in spirit and truth, for such the Father seeks to worship him' (John 4: 23).

To worship 'in spirit' does not mean to worship without rites and ceremonies, although in the past some groups of Christians have interpreted the verse in that way. It means to worship under the impulse of the Holy Spirit. To worship 'in truth' is to respond to God as the One who has revealed the truth about himself and his kingdom through Jesus Christ. The absolution and the peace are the liturgy's way of helping us to prepare our hearts to worship in spirit and in truth.

The eucharist reaches its first climax in the passages of the Bible which are read to us. The Old Testament reading tells us how God chose the people of Israel and prepared them for the manifestation of himself in Jesus Christ. The reading from the gospels unfolds for us the story of the Messiah's birth, life, ministry, death, resurrection and ascension. The readings from Acts and the epistles teach us about the gift of the Holy Spirit and the response of the apostolic Church to the Gospel of the kingdom.

The readings are expounded in the sermon, in mime, drama and dance, and in hymns and songs. But the readings are focal. Quite often some of the passages will be very familiar to us. We discuss them in Bible study-groups or in some Christian educational project. We use them in our private prayers.

Yet within the context of worship the passages have a new authority. Through the Spirit they bring us the voice of God. All we've learned about them suddenly becomes submissive to this ministry of the Word. Once again we are made aware of 'the living and abiding Word of God' (1 Pet. 1: 24). It can be a moment in which the presence of Christ is very real to us.

The recitation of the creed is a reaffirmation of our personal commitment to the teaching of the scriptures. Individually we may go through periods of doubting and questioning. Sometimes belief may seem difficult. Yet the liturgy shepherds us into the traditional Christian response to the revelation of God in Jesus Christ which the Bible enshrines. It is in the faith pronounced by the creed that we were baptised; it is in that faith we want to continue. We demonstrate that by standing with the Church and reciting it together.

To be a disciple of Jesus Christ is to be united with him in his concern for the poor, the suffering, the needy and the oppressed. Our unity with his concern is expressed liturgically in the general intercession. One with him as our priestly advocate and mediator, we bring before the throne of grace the needs of the Church and of the world.

On certain days we concentrate on specific issues – the Third World in Christian Aid Week and the reunion of the Church during the Unity Octave. But the intercessions offered during the eucharist are intended to be *general* – that is, for the whole human family. Our private concerns can be tossed in like the stick thrown into the river, but they are carried along by the overall prayer for the Church and the world. The arrangement of the intercessions in the service-books provides us with a pattern for this.

Intercession and discipleship, therefore, go hand-in-hand. To pray for others is to be committed to seeking an answer to that prayer ourselves in the will of God. It involves us in God's response to the request. We do not pray and then stand aside to see if the Lord answers that petition; we pray and then in the Spirit offer ourselves to God for him to use us in his response.

For some situations there is little we can do except pray. We may intercede for the Church in China for many years and do no more except keep ourselves informed of what is happening there.

For other situations we can make some contribution. Intercessions for Christian Aid Week ought to include a review of our own personal giving to Third World projects. Covenanted subscriptions to such bodies are signs that we are endeavouring in a tiny way to adjust the imbalance in the distribution of wealth in our world. We can also learn about the work of the agency as well and share in its local activities.

And for a few situations we can help in a very practical way or exert personal influence. Most congregations pray for some sick people by name. Are those sick visited? They also pray for the spread of God's kingdom in the neighbourhood. Have we accepted a personal responsibility for evangelism in the ministry of the local church? If we are not involved in seeking a solution to the problems about which we pray, we are making ourselves part of those problems.

Usually during the general intercession there is a period of silence. This reminds us that the people and events we name in our prayers are named for our benefit rather than God's. With him all hearts are completely open, all desires are fully known, and from him no secrets are hid. We do not have to come to him with a shopping-list. He knows that we are agonizing for the dying child and its parents and that we feel helpless in our concern for the starving nation. Although naming people and events are important in our prayers, silence may be even more important sometimes, for it is then that we are more likely to hear God telling us what he wants us to do about those for whom we pray.

At the end of the intercessions we move towards the second climax of the service, the ministry of the sacrament. The bread and the wine are placed upon the altar. The earlier notes of praise and thanksgiving in the hymns and the Gloria come together in a crescendo in the eucharistic prayer, the thanksgiving.

'Lift up your hearts!' cries the president.

'We lift them to the Lord!' we reply.

The prayer recalls the saving events for which we praise God, sometimes with reference to the festival or the occasion we are commemorating. The scriptural texts and themes weave in and out of the prayer like the subjects in the movements of a great symphony. The president's words are punctuated with acclamations from the congregation: 'Holy, holy, holy Lord' – 'Christ will come again!' – 'Blessing and honour and glory!'

Into the prayer comes the narrative of the Last Supper. What we are celebrating is the new covenant God has established with his people through the death and resurrection of his Son Jesus Christ: 'This is my blood of the new covenant, which is poured out for many' (Mark 14: 24). Through it we are being summoned to present ourselves 'as a living sacrifice, holy and acceptable to God, which is your spiritual worship' (Rom. 12: 1).

Sometimes I follow the text as the president reads it in a book. At other times I stand or kneel letting the prayer flow through me as I lift my thoughts and feelings to God. When the president reaches the words which ask God to send his Holy Spirit on the bread and the wine and on the worshippers, I make an act of faith that I am once more being plunged (baptised) in the Spirit. Then to the communion rail.

'The Body of Christ . . . the Blood of Christ keep you in eternal life.'

The meals which Jesus shared with his disciples after his resurrection, especially the supper on the road to Emmaus, are suddenly made present. And all that meals mean to me – especially meals with family and friends – in refreshment and fellowship converge on that moment. On occasions I have joined in a celebration of the eucharist in a home during a meal round a table. I can see the practical difficulties for many congregations in celebrating regularly in this manner, yet I think every communicant should have the experience from time to time. It makes the eucharists we celebrate in churches so much more meaningful.

'For as often as you eat this bread and drink the cup, you proclaim the Lord's death until he comes' (1 Cor. 11: 26). The new covenant, sealed in the sacrifice on the cross, becomes a visible and tangible reality in our midst. Although we receive Christ by faith when we take the bread and the wine, the reception does not depend on the quality of our faith. In the sacrament is an assured, covenanted presence of Christ. By his Spirit God reaches out to us through the sacramental sign. We can relax and surrender to him, knowing that now – as always – the initiative comes from him.

Sometimes other sacramental signs are added to the bread and the wine – the washing of water and the laying-on of hands in baptism and confirmation, the joining of hands and the exchange of vows in marriage, the laying-on of hands in ordination, the anointing with oil for healing. As God took human nature to show what is possible through his grace for all human beings, so he takes created things in the liturgy and shows what is possible by his Spirit when we are united with him.

Belief in the presence of Christ in the eucharist encourages us to believe in his presence in our lives. 'I am the bread of life; he who comes to me shall not hunger, and he who believes in me shall never thirst' (John 6: 35). Holy Communion brings the Body of Christ to us as manna for our pilgrimage. The liturgy offers us a renewing of our discipleship.

Around us at the communion rail are people at all sorts of different stages on their pilgrimage. That is what gives the service its varied significance. It can mean one thing to us one week, another thing the next week.

In its report, *Your Kingdom Come,* the World Council of Churches put it this way:

There are times and places where the very act of coming together to celebrate the eucharist can be a public witness. In certain states Christians may be discouraged from attending such worship or penalised for it. We hear of those who come together at great risk, and whose courage reveals to those around them how precious is this sacrament. In other situations the eucharist may be an open-air witness so planned that many may see it. There is, at the Lord's table, a vision of God which draws the human heart to the Lord . . .

Each Christian minister and congregation has to seek this

understanding, and we can only give some indications: where a people is being harshly oppressed, the eucharist speaks of the exodus or deliverance from bondage. Where Christians are rejected or imprisoned for their faith, the bread and wine become the life of the Lord who was rejected by men but has become the chief stone of the corner. Where the church sees a diminishing membership and its budgets depressing, the eucharist declares that there are no limits to God's giving and no end to hope in him. Where discrimination by race, sex or class is a danger for the community, the eucharist enables people of all sorts to partake of the one food and to be made one people. Where people are affluent and at ease with life, the eucharist says, 'As Christ shares his life, share what you have with the hungry.' Where a congregation is isolated by politics or war or geography, the eucharist unites us with all God's people in all places and all ages. Where a sister or brother is near death, the eucharist becomes a doorway into the kingdom of our loving Father.[1]

We leave the communion rail and then we are dismissed into God's world to take the part he has reserved for us in his mission.

There is another aspect of our Christian pilgrimage that the eucharist renews: it points us to our ultimate destiny in the kingdom of God.

'I have earnestly desired to eat this passover with you before I suffer,' said Jesus to his disciples, 'for I tell you I shall never eat it again until it is fulfilled in the kingdom of God' (Luke 22: 15–16).

The kingdom of God breaks through into this life where men and women are obedient to his will, but it will not be revealed in its fullness until the world has ended. We are sojourners as well as citizens in this life. This is a necessary corrective. It is so easy to become engrossed in the affairs of the kingdom here and now that we forget we are destined for 'the kingdom prepared for you from the foundation of the world' (Matt. 25: 34). The liturgy adjusts the balance for us.

One of the ways it does this is by handing on the tradition of fasting before receiving Communion. This discipline has its roots in the scriptures. Jesus fasted, and he encouraged his disciples to fast. From one angle fasting is an expression of penitence for sin. That is how it became associated with abstinence on Fridays and in the seasons of Advent and Lent. Fasting, praying and alms-giving are the traditional signs of an amendment of life.

But that is a somewhat negative angle on fasting. A more positive angle is to see a fast as a putting on of the armour of God, as a gesture of protest against the principalities and powers which have been overcome by the triumph of the cross. The use of the fast as a moral and political protest is well known from news bulletins. By fasting the disciple indicates his willingness to reject the world, the flesh and the devil, and to align himself with the suffering and victory of Jesus Christ. Fasting looks forward to the time when we shall no longer require the food of this existence to sustain us.

The eucharistic fast has fallen into disuse nowadays with the relaxation of Church discipline. There was always a danger it would become an objective in itself detached from its inner significance. The attitude sometimes got around that the most important preparation for Communion was to go without breakfast! But there has been a renewal of fasting among Christians of all denominations on specific occasions, and the spiritual strengths of the discipline are being rediscovered.

In the liturgy itself we are reminded of the end of our pilgrimage in various ways.

First, it makes us aware that in worship we are sharing with the whole Church in heaven as well as on earth. We praise God 'with angels and archangels and all the company of heaven.' The Book of Revelation, which unveils prophetically truths about the end of the ages, provides much of the symbolism and language of worship. A glance through its pages shows how much hymns and prayers have quarried from it.

Second, the liturgy commemorates the witness of saints and martyrs through the ages and thanks God for their example. The visit of Pope John Paul II to Canterbury Cathedral in 1982 was a moving celebration of the fact that martyrdom is not a spiritual gift belonging to distance centuries. It is said that more Christians have died for their faith in the twentieth century than in all the previous ones. TV viewers saw the faces of Maximilian Kolbe, Dietrich Bonhoeffer, Janani Luwum, Maria Skobtsova, Martin Luther King and Oscar Romero superimposed on the flames of the candles lit in the Chapel of Saints and Martyrs of Our Own Time, and heard the Pope read the collect for All Saints:

> Give us grace so to follow your blessed saints and martyrs
> in all virtuous and godly living,
> that we may come to those unspeakable joys
> which you have prepared for those who truly love you;
> through Jesus Christ our Lord.

With this commemoration we also remember those who have died. 'Welcome into your kingdom our departed brothers and sisters, and all who have left this world in your friendship,' says Eucharistic Prayer III of the Roman rite.

Third, the liturgy give us affirmations of faith in the second coming of Christ. This is the theme of the season of Advent, although it tends to be swamped by the preparations for Christmas. In the creed we say, 'He will come again in glory to judge the living and the dead, and his kingdom will have no end.' And in one of the acclamations in the eucharistic prayer, we are encouraged to shout, 'Christ will come again!'

Fourth, the liturgy helps us to prepare for our own deaths. Admittedly, this element is not as strong in contemporary

services – perhaps reflecting the modern attitude that death
is the great unmentionable – although the custom is still
maintained in some churches of ceremonially marking the
foreheads of communicants with ashes on Ash Wednesday
with the admonition, 'Remember, O man, that thou art dust,
and unto dust shalt thou return.'

The ancient preface from the requiem mass has been
retained and given a new dress in the funeral service of the
Alternative Service Book, linking the death of a relative or
friend with the promises of the New Testament:

And now we give you thanks
because through him
you have given us the hope of a glorious resurrection,
so that although death comes to us all,
yet we rejoice in the promise of eternal life;
for to your faithful people life is changed, not taken away,
and when our mortal flesh is laid aside,
an everlasting dwelling-place is made ready for us in heaven . . .

So, then, if the eucharist looks back to the Last Supper
and to the meals which the risen Christ shared with his
astonished disciples, it also looks forward to the banquet of
the kingdom of God depicted in Christ's parables. This is the
heart of the Christian hope. 'When I go and prepare a place
for you, I will come again and take you to myself, that where
I am you may be also' (John 14: 3). Jesus Christ is the
pioneer of our faith in that he has gone before us and been
through all that faces us. He is the perfecter of our faith in
that all that is lacking in us he will provide out of the riches
of his grace.

Death and resurrection is the end of our pilgrimage, the
fulfilment of our discipleship, in the mercy of God.

Fear of dying is natural enough. Perhaps it is the thought
of the pain we might be subjected to rather than the process
of dying itself which alarms us (although medical care has

done much to make the process of dying comparatively painless these days).

As for the process itself, we know that when we fall asleep in death, there will be no waking in a strange place. We shall find the Father who made us and who loves us, and the Christ for whom we have been searching and in whose Spirit we have been following. There, too, we shall find the people of God with whom we are for ever united. Much will be familiar in heaven through our experience of God's kingdom in this life.

Sadness at the prospect of dying is natural enough, too. Personally I shall be sad at being separated (if only for a while) from those I love. I shall regret that I shall not see my family grow up. I shall be sorry that the beauty of this creation in all its varied forms will be taken away from me.

But in the resurrection there will be so much to wonder at and to praise God for. With many Christians, I believe that the kingdom of God will embrace everything which is good and beautiful in this creation. The evolution of the universe as we know it seems to point forward to a new creation of which this world is but a dim foreshadowing. If it is God's purpose to unite all things in Christ, things on earth as well as things in heaven, then nothing which is truly of him in this life will be lost or wasted. When we die, we can look forward to awakening in a paradise, a garden, in which all the natural goodness and beauty of this universe has been transfigured by the hand of God.

And I believe no human love will be lost, either. The fact that I have loved someone, or that someone has loved me, will be consummated in the fullness of God's eternal love. If human love in this life is a preparation for understanding divine love, then we shall experience that human affection again in its purest form in heaven.

The aged parent who died years ago, the only child who was lost so tragically, the husband or wife who passed away unexpectedly in the prime of life, the friend killed in his youth in a road accident – those relationships will not vanish. Cleansed and enriched by the Holy Spirit, they will be part of the network of relationships which we shall enjoy in the kingdom of God.

And what of ourselves? Is it frivolous to speculate about our resurrection body?

Paul didn't think so. He treated the question with the utmost seriousness and confidence. 'For this perishable nature must put on the imperishable, and this mortal nature must put on immortality' (I Cor. 15: 53). Jesus spoke of being as the angels in heaven.

But in spite of these hints in the New Testament, we have to admit that we know nothing of this mystery. God has withheld the answer to the question from us. Perhaps nothing of the loveliness of our human life will be lost. Perhaps in our resurrection body we shall be given something of every age we have lived – the age when our childhood flowered, the age when we were happiest, the age when we reached our fullest powers, the age when we were most faithful to our truest love.

> No more shall there be in it
> an infant that lives but a few days,
> or an old man who does not fill out his days,
> for the child shall die a hundred years old (Isa. 65. 20).

To live by the Spirit prepares us to die in the Spirit, and in the Spirit to be raised in Christ. 'If the Spirit of him who raised Jesus from the dead dwells in you, he who raised Christ Jesus from the dead will give life to your mortal bodies also through his Spirit which dwells in you' (Rom. 8: 11).

So we shall come to the kingdom of our God. And, as Bishop Ignatius of Antioch said on his way to martyrdom in Rome, 'When I arrive there, I shall be a real man.'

---

[1] World Council of Churches, *Your Kingdom Come* (1974), pp. 205-6.

JESUS & CHRISTIAN ORIGINS OUTSIDE THE NEW TESTAMENT

F. F. Bruce

What collateral proof outside the New Testament is there for the historical existence of Jesus Christ? If the Bible account of his activities is accurate he would have aroused sufficient interest to feature in other historical records of the time.

F. F. Bruce has studied these records in detail. He draws from a variety of Jewish, pagan, apocryphal and Islamic writings of the New Testament period, and refers also to the Dead Sea Scrolls, the Gospel of Thomas and the Koran. Every important source is considered in the discussion, and archaeological evidence is taken into full account.

The collected material makes fascinating reading alongside the first-hand information available in the New Testament.

THE HARD SAYINGS
OF JESUS

F. F. Bruce

There are two kinds of hard sayings in the Gospels, according to F. F. Bruce: those that are difficult to understand; and those that are easy to comprehend, but all too difficult to put into practice. Seventy of these sayings are explored in detail in this magnificent study.

'Dr. F. F. Bruce, one of the most distinguished British New Testament scholars, has set the tone to which other writers in the series will aspire. His book is characterised by clarity, honesty, scholarship, intelligibility, and faith. I know of no book like this, and I am confident that it will reach a very wide circle of readers. The considered fruits of his research and reflection will afford both understanding and confidence to many, and will bring the person of Jesus into clearer focus for every reader.' *Michael Green*

PENTECOSTAL ANGLICANS

John Gunstone

The charismatic movement has swept powerfully through church fellowships. Individuals have been revitalised, and now the question is being asked: how does this affect our denominations?

In the Church of England, former spiritual gifts, fossilised in customs and offices, are being restored: new ministries are taking their place beside older ones. But it is not simply a matter of dry bones being brought back to life, argues John Gunstone: the Church of England is being challenged to change many things, not least some that she regards as 'glories of the Anglican tradition'. Her concept of what it means to be Christian, and what it means to be the Church of Jesus Christ in today's world, is being revolutionised.

A PEOPLE FOR HIS PRAISE

John Gunstone

Despite the flood of literature on the charismatic movement, little has been written about the problems it has raised in local churches. It has brought acknowledged benefits, but there is still suspicion and misunderstanding. Charismatics have found it difficult to relate their personal experience of the Holy Spirit to the on-going worship and life of their congregation.

'I have begun,' writes John Gunstone, 'with the problems that arise between an individual and the congregation when he or she is baptised in the Spirit. Then I have looked at a congregation as a creation of the Spirit and suggested ways in which individuals and groups can prepare for renewal within it. From this I have gone on to show how the charismatic movement can enrich the life and worship of a congregation, its leadership, its ministry and its mission in the neighbourhood.'